THE MERGING OF TITANS

A History of the Law Firm that Bears Their Names

Edward L. Cuddihy

Jaeckle Fleischmann & Mugel, LLP
Buffalo, N.Y.

Published by Jaeckle Fleischmann & Mugel, LLP,
12 Fountain Plaza, Buffalo, NY 14202-2292.

Printed by Petit Printing, Buffalo, N.Y., U.S.A.
Layout and Design by Jim Bitten
This book was published and printed in Buffalo, N.Y., U.S.A.

Library of Congress Control Number: 2007937168

Includes bibliographical references and index.

ISBN: 978-0-615-16282-9

Contents

Foreword by William I. Schapiro   5

Author's Note   7

Chapter I
Introduction: The Firm with Three Unpronounceable Names   9

Chapter II
Edwin F. Jaeckle: From Humble Beginnings   15

Chapter III
The Fleischmann Brothers: Designed for Success   25

Chapter IV
Jaeckle: Ten Years in the National Spotlight   37

Chapter V
Manly Fleischmann: A Star on the National Stage   57

Chapter VI
The Group of 13: The Founding Partners   69

Chapter VII
The Sum of the Parts Times Ten   85

Chapter VIII
Epilogue   105

Appendix I: *Firm Genealogy*   113

Appendix II: *Jaeckle's Political Timeline*   114

Appendix III: *The Education of Manly Fleischmann*   115

Appendix IV: *Firm's Partners as of 2007*   118

Sources   126

Footnotes   127

Index   132

Eight Pages of Photos   following 64

Foreword

In April 1955, two Buffalo law firms merged to create the firm then known as Jaeckle, Fleischmann, Kelly, Swart and Augspurger. Each of the lawyers in the firm's new name had earned considerable stature in the region's legal community. Moreover, Edwin F. Jaeckle and Manly Fleischmann, the two lawyers who respectively headed each of the constituent firms, were widely recognized well beyond Buffalo and Western New York.

Ed Cuddihy, who combines the talents of a biographer, journalist and historian, now tells the story of these two lawyers, their partners and the law firm they created and how they served their communities, their nation and their profession. In the following pages, Ed gives us meaningful insights into their personal standards, their sense of service to their community, state and nation, and their triumphs and disappointments. This personal history is presented in the context of a region and nation energized by several centuries of immigration and challenged by foreign wars and major political, social and economic issues.

Our firm's name is now Jaeckle Fleischmann & Mugel, LLP. The third name refers to our late partner Albert R. Mugel, who, as you will learn in the following pages, was a brilliant tax and estates lawyer who also imparted his knowledge in that field to successive generations of students at the University at Buffalo Law School (and, among other accomplishments, served his country on the battlefield as a tank commander in both World War II and the Korean War).

This book was conceived by James J. Tanous, a former partner and Executive Committee Chairman of our firm, and Randall M. Odza, a partner in our Labor and Employment Practice Group, as a means to inform our present lawyers about the origins of our firm and the accomplishments and character of the partners who are no longer with us. We are grateful to them for initiating this effort and to Ed Cuddihy for this informative and highly readable work. As is true of any responsible law firm, we endeavor to merge the wisdom and experience of our predecessors with that of our own to serve our clients, our profession and our community.

We are pleased to share this history with clients and friends of our firm.

William I. Schapiro,
Partner and past Executive Committee Chairman

Author's Note

A publisher I used to work for was fond of saying: Sometimes you go out for popcorn and come back with peanuts…and that isn't always a bad thing.

I can only hope it isn't always bad, because I feel a little like I've been sent on the popcorn errand following my research of the history of the law firm Jaeckle, Fleischmann & Mugel. I set out seeking a grand starting point, a day somewhere in 1955 when Edwin F. Jaeckle and Manly Fleischmann stood at the threshold of their new offices in the Rand Building in Downtown Buffalo, shook hands, patted each other on the back, and began a relationship that would carry them through the rest of their lives. It would be even better if the pair had unveiled that bronze-lettered plaque that faces visitors when the elevator opens on the 8th floor of 12 Fountain Plaza.

Well, not only is there no such day in 1955, but it didn't happen that way. Just as the history of the American republic doesn't begin with the signing of the Declaration of Independence on July 4, 1776, but stretches back at least 150 years before that monumental date, neither does the history of Jaeckle Fleischmann begin with a merger of law firms in 1955. There may be some significance to the post-War year of 1955, a time when Buffalo already had reached its apex as an industrial giant and one of the nation's largest population centers, but it is not the starting point for this story. This story begins in the first decades of the 20th Century, during the formative years of the two men – one born in 1894, the other in 1908 – who would not only lend their names to the firm, but whose characters still are evidenced daily at 12 Fountain Plaza nearly a century later.

So this is the story of the individuals who molded the firm, who they were and how they got to be who they became.

Acknowledgements:

Because the number of persons with direct and personal knowledge of the founders is limited by the passing of the years, I must acknowledge that a large portion of this work is based on secondary sources. By far, the lion's share of the research into these sources was carried out by Irene E. Cuddihy, Ph.D., who sifted through 50 years of the *New York Times* and *Washington Post* archives, along with the archives of several national magazines, among them *Time* and *Harper's*, documenting the public lives of the founders. In addition, Richard Norton Smith's definitive biography of Thomas E. Dewey, *Thomas E. Dewey* *and His Time*s, proved an invaluable resource for Jaeckle's political years.

David Valenzuela, library director at *The Buffalo News*, and Sara Paulson and Amy Yakawiak of his staff supplied a wealth of information from the archives of *The Buffalo News* and its predecessor, *The Buffalo Evening News*. The archives of the *Buffalo Courier-Express* and the *Buffalo Times* were not as easy to access, and would have been impossible without the assistance of the staffs at the local history room of the Buffalo & Erie County Library, and the Buffalo & Erie County Historical Society. Also assisting was Mark Lozo of the Theodore Roosevelt Inaugural National Historic Site. A special thanks goes to John Neville, a friend and top-flight editor, for the time and patience he accorded the manuscript.

Many individuals, both inside the firm and outside it, gave freely of their time to sit for hours of interviews. Foremost among them were Adelbert Fleischmann, who at 93 years old, searched his memory and his files, with the help of Susan Migaj, for answers to my unending questions. Erma Jaeckle, who Edwin married after the death of his first wife, Grace, added a dimension to the Jaeckle chapters. Alison Fleischmann, Manly's only daughter, not only filled in Fleischmann family blanks, but kindly gave me access to family scrapbooks for the project. Ilene Fleischmann, Adelbert's daughter-in-law, also added to the Fleischmann material.

William I. Schapiro shared his more than 40 years with the firm, and Paul Weaver and Randall M. Odza were not far behind in the number of years and memories they shared. Others who generously shared their time and thoughts were Ralph L. Halpern, James J. Tanous, Edward G. Piwowarczyk, Michele O. Heffernan, Joseph P. Kubarek, Mitchell J. Banas Jr., Heath J. Szymczak and J. Montieth (Monty) Estes. Founding partners John Wick and J.B. Walsh contributed to the early years of the firm, as did Richard Mugel, the son of Albert Mugel; Ann Tierney, the daughter of Larry Wagner; Monsignor James G. Kelly, the son of Harry Kelly; Mrs. John G. Putnam Jr., wife of John Putnam; Michael Swart, son of Joseph Swart; Timothy Leixner, a former partner; Meghan M. McDonnell, Scott P. Horton, Cathy Kotas, Susan Migaj and Ali Owczarkowski of the Jaeckle Fleischmann staff. Douglas Turner of the Washington Bureau of *The Buffalo News*, and George Borrelli, retired political reporter for *The News*, shared their recollections of the firm's founders.

Without the assistance of all these persons, the history of Jaeckle Fleischmann & Mugel would have been little more than a collection of names and dates.

CHAPTER I

Introduction:
The Firm with Three Unpronounceable Names

It is inconceivable in Buffalo, New York, the very definition of a large city that feels small town, that a major homespun business which has maintained headquarters within shouting distance of City Hall for more than half a century should be unknown to the vast majority of its inhabitants.

But that's the case with the law firm commonly known as Jaeckle Fleischmann.

It becomes even more implausible when one considers that this firm has been a part of Buffalo's fabric through the mid-20th Century and into the 21st Century. Whether it be through the hospital systems and the health insurers that pave one's way into this world or the life insurance and cemetery companies that note one's passing from it, this group of lawyers has put its stamp on the life cycle of the community.

When you use electric power, when you fill your tank with gasoline, when you shop for canned vegetables or soft cookies, when you work or worship in a structure constructed by a local contractor, when you use public transportation, or when you build the cars that travel the nation's highways, you unknowingly are a beneficiary of actions of the law firm that always has chosen to maintain a low profile, to remain in the background of the city's life.

Members of this firm have practiced under two firm names since its formation in 1955, and another dozen names before that, but common to each of the official titles has been the names Jaeckle and Fleischmann, the accepted shorthand in legal circles for Edwin F. Jaeckle and Manly Fleischmann, the two highest profile founders who placed their impermeable mark on the organization they nurtured.

The names of Augspurger, Kelly, Swart and Mugel – all names from the firm's letterhead – are names from the past, as are Ed Jaeckle and Manly Fleischmann, but the spirit and character of the firm's two most prominent founders remain like threads woven into the fiber of the city.

Ed Jaeckle and Manly Fleischmann were known by a generation of Buffalo business and corporate leaders as men who thrived on hard work, who were honest and open to a fault, and who always looked to the long haul, not only to their own interests and the interests of their clients, but to the larger interests of the community. The Jaeckle and Fleischmann tradition dies hard. Fifteen years after Ed Jaeckle's death, it is common to see the names of members of the firm on the region's cultural boards and not-for-profit foundations, just as the names Jaeckle and Fleischmann had been two decades earlier.

And to be sure, the characters of these two national figures didn't mysteriously spring to life and harden strong one day in 1955 at Main and Lafayette Square. Both these men had fashioned their strengths over decades. The year 1955 marked the height of the post-war era when belching smokestacks attested to a prosperous city with its undercurrent of wealth. South Buffalo had its smokestacks, as did Lackawanna, Tonawanda, Black Rock and the East Side. In fact, the entire Erie-Niagara shoreline from Lackawanna, through the cities of Buffalo and Tonawanda, to Niagara Falls was flush with industry, much of it homegrown. And wherever there was industry, there were clients for a law firm specializing in corporate law, estate planning and taxes.

Ed Jaeckle and Manly Fleischmann had come from two different eras in the history of metropolitan Buffalo. Their skills were honed in the national spotlight, but on two different stages. And they came together at a time and place that made eminent good sense in the fulfilling of their ambitions.

For the elder Ed Jaeckle, it was the hard work, never-give-up values of Buffalo's industrious German-American Fruit Belt that surrounded him as a youth and young man. For Manly Fleischmann, it was the Fleischmann family values absorbed in the Village of Hamburg that remained with him throughout his life. The six Fleischmann brothers shared a heritage that was an unusual amalgam of old-world culture, Jewish drive and wanderlust, and down-to-earth American Quakerism.

When one talks about Jaeckle Fleischmann & Mugel, the late 20th Century and early 21st Century partnership name, one envisions a cadre of 70 to 80 lawyers, plus supporting staff, spread over two floors of one of Main Street's major office buildings. One can picture the bold, brass san-serif letters on the dark walnut plaque and the chrome telescope aimed at the waterfront that nourished this city. One thinks of banking and insurance, aerospace research and heavy industry, investment trusts and family foundations. The Amherst, Rochester and Arizona satellite offices come to mind, as does the unprecedented promoting of nine associates to the level of partner at one time in the Fall of 2006. It has all the hallmarks of a large, flourishing 21st Century business.

But to understand the character of the firm, one must envision Ed Jaeckle handling wills and property transfers from his modest frame home on Lemon Street, and Manly Fleischmann living hand to mouth in post-war New York City. One pictures Ed Jaeckle holding court at the end of a large table at the Buffalo Club, entertaining all comers with his tales of cut-throat national politics. Or it's the image of Manly and his brother Adelbert Fleischmann, with John Stenger, on a Saturday afternoon in the Tap Room at the Lafayette Hotel, dissecting some arcane legal principle behind state condemnation proceedings or just discussing the status of American Airlines or the Equitable Life Assurance Society.

It is the firm with three names that no one can spell correctly – no less pronounce – the firm operating under the iron hand of Ed Jaeckle and the legal acumen of Manly Fleischmann. But Ed Jaeckle's firm hand could be seen decades earlier, dragging the last vote out of an East Side tavern in the 1920s, and the logical Fleischmann thought process was built on years of discipline, culminating in the deadly training of spies to infiltrate the Japanese lines in Burma during World War II. In the period in between were the years when a young firm considered, but mercifully never aired, a radio jingle set to the tune of a popular soft-drink commercial that went:

> Jaeckle Fleischmann hits the spot,
> Fourteen partners, that's a lot;
> Twice as much for your money too,
> Jaeckle Fleischmann is the firm for you![1]

An astute observer of the Buffalo scene might know that Jaeckle Fleischmann was involved in the three most noteworthy local litigations of the era: The Love Canal environmental disaster, the Attica Prison riot fallout of the Rockefeller years, and Erie County's domed stadium saga. All three fell into the magic legal category that Manly Fleischmann used to describe as "enticing vistas of endless litigation."[2]

Less known is that Ed Jaeckle was one of the principal lawyers in the estimated $700 million sale of the Statler Hotel chain to Conrad Hilton's interests
in 1954. At that time, the deal was believed to be among the largest business
transactions in the nation's history. [3]

Few know that Jaeckle Fleischmann lawyers guided the transformation of
the old private Niagara Frontier Transit System into the regional transportation
authority we know today as the NFTA. It had been Ed Jaeckle's transportation
dream for Buffalo as early as the Gov. Thomas E. Dewey era to have the old
bankrupt IRC reorganized into a regional transportation authority. But that
dream would have to wait several decades that would include Jaeckle
Fleischmann representing the winning side in a bitter proxy battle over the bus
company before the state would finally create the regional transportation
authority to oversee public transit and airline traffic in and out of Buffalo-
Niagara.

And even less known is that in 1977 when legendary Omaha investor
Warren E. Buffett purchased *The Buffalo Evening News*, the city's leading
media outlet, from the founding Butler family, Jaeckle Fleischmann lawyers
played the lead role.

Ed Jaeckle's political savvy had been recognized in the national media for
a decade as he engineered victories for his candidate at state and national conventions while never capturing the big prize, but fifty years after his retirement
from politics, only the shadows of a major political career remain in the memories of an aging generation. And a few old-timers can tell you that after World
War II, Manly Fleischmann was called the third most powerful man in
Washington, behind President Truman and his secretary of state, but fewer yet
can tell you why. [4]

Yet, to a generation of Buffalo business leaders, Ed Jaeckle and Manly
Fleischmann were the voices of common sense. They were the men whose
trusted counsel went far beyond the scope of Fleischmann's formidable knowledge of the law and Jaeckle's celebrated list of high-level contacts. What they
had in abundance was the quality of down-to-earth sound judgment, the quality
of wisdom that would guide a client and his company through the everyday
obstacles onto a straight-arrow course for the future. They were the unnamed
architects of many a business plan, the unseen mentors, the trusted and reliable
friends.

To comprehend the character of the firm that has come down to the 21st Century as Jaeckle Fleischmann & Mugel, LLP, one must understand and appreciate its underpinnings, its foundation. Even so, Ed Jaeckle and Manly Fleischmann would be the first to tell any reader that the firm was not built on two men, it was built on the expertise and work of many men and women who the industry likes to refer to as "last-word lawyers." The founders expressed that sentiment over and over during their lifetimes. So to understand the firm, one needs to look at many people, some living and some deceased.

But all agree the firm was built on the strength of two titans. So this is primarily the story of Edwin F. Jaeckle and Manly Fleischmann, the story of their lives, the story of the fires that forged their characters, the story of those who most affected their decisions, and the story of the firm that bears their names.

CHAPTER II

Edwin F. Jaeckle:
From Humble Beginnings

When Jacob and Mary Marx Jaeckle gave birth to a son on Oct. 27, 1894, and named him Edwin Frederick Jaeckle, they well might have anticipated that young Edwin, the second generation of American-born Jaeckles, would follow his father into carpentry and eventually, if Jacob's hopes blossomed to fruition, young Edwin might inherit the family construction business.

Jacob had been born on American soil in the 1850s, the son of German immigrants from the Black Forest region. Mary Marx's parents had come to this bustling city at the western end of the Erie Canal from the Hesse Darmstadt region of Germany.

Both the Jaeckle and Marx families had sought to fulfill their dreams through the great immigration of 1840 and they settled in an area of orchards and vegetable gardens north of the core city of Buffalo and east of Main Street. Eventually, a series of streets with names like Grape, Peach, Orange, Maple, Spruce and Lemon were laid out among the orchards and that immigrant community began to be called the Fruit Belt by the generation of more established Buffalonians who lived west of Main Street.

This German community, bounded roughly by Michigan Avenue on the west and Jefferson Avenue on the east, and pushing north from Genesee Street would eventually be home to nearly 10,000 residents and would bear the name "Fruit Belt" right into the 21st Century, despite its bifurcation with the construction of the Kensington Expressway. Jacob Jaeckle had been born on Spruce Street and his wife on nearby Sycamore Street. [1]

By the time of Edwin's birth, the Fruit Belt was a prosperous immigrant neighborhood in one of the nation's booming cities. Edwin was born in the 2-story frame house at 26 Lemon St., near Genesee, built by his father. Jacob, a planning-mill owner, also built St. Peter's United Evangelical Church, where the family would worship, and later he would build Masten Park High School, where Edwin would be graduated after he attended Public School 37 at Carlton and Peach streets. In later years, Ed Jaeckle would say of his parents and neighbors: "They were just good, hearty German-Americans who worked like hell." [2]

It was his mother, Mary, who encouraged young Jaeckle to go into law. Mary had befriended a neighborhood lawyer named Robert F. Schelling, probably through her husband's Pan American Exposition projects. Jacob, who died when Ed Jaeckle was in his teens, is credited with constructing three of the pavilions at the Pan American Exposition in Delaware Park, and Schelling was part of a group of attorneys who represented the 1901 exposition. In January of 1902, after the assassination of President William McKinley and a financially disappointing exposition, Schelling reportedly brokered the deal to sell a group of Pan American buildings to the Chicago Wrecking Co. for $80,000.

Edwin went directly to the University of Buffalo Law School, upon his graduation from Masten Park, and his mother arranged for him to clerk for Robert Schelling. Ed told his colleague Ralph Halpern many years later that to the young clerk's great embarrassment, Schelling's secretary insisted on counting out his two dollars a week wage in front of the other staffers. It is said that Schelling had young Jaeckle check with his mother before agreeing to that handsome wage. [3]

Tuition in 1915 at the law school was only $50 a year. UB's Law School consisted of two offices in the Ellicott Square Building, a prestigious location considering that this structure had been the nation's largest office building when it was constructed on Main Street in Downtown Buffalo. The Law School had one paid instructor, Dean Carlos Alden, and a cadre of volunteer lecturers, attorneys who often didn't show up for class. One office served as the law library and the other, the classroom for the 24 members of Ed Jaeckle's graduating class of 1915. [4]

Upon being admitted to the bar, Jaeckle joined Schelling's practice and when Schelling died in 1916, Jaeckle continued in practice with Edward J. Garono. Jaeckle would still be associated with the older Garono right into the 1950s. In the 20s, they joined up with the firm of Palmer, Hauck & Wickser, and in the 30s, Jaeckle and Garono left to become partners with Carleton Ladd in Ladd, Garono & Jaeckle. And in the 50s, it would be Garono, Jaeckle, Kelly & Wick, with the addition of Harry Kelly and Charles J. Wick, followed almost immediately by the further addition of Joseph Swart, and another name change.

Decades later, Jaeckle would be known as the consummate rainmaker but not so in those early years. Jaeckle told an anonymous writer for the *UB Law Forum* in 1986 that after graduation, he earned $8 a week working for Schelling, and being close to downtown and the only lawyer in the neighborhood, Jaeckle would often work right out of the family's Lemon Street home.

"It was simple then…. I'd close a real estate deal, draw up a will, get the paperwork for a license or handle some simple litigation – nothing of consequence. I'd charge a dollar or two," Jaeckle said. [5]

A generation later, when law partner Larry Wagner would drive his family out the Kensington Expressway toward the airport, Wagner would point north and tell his daughter Anne: "There's Ed's old house." By 2007, 26 Lemon St., with its red brick front and white porch pillars, looked a little rough at the edges but was one of a handful of original homes remaining on the street. Most of the other large 2 - story frame houses, bearing the telltale high roofs, decorative eaves and attic windows of their German-American origin, had burned in arson fires or just had been left to deteriorate. Some had been replaced with modular housing which was giving new life to this changing neighborhood behind Buffalo's Medical Corridor in the 21st Century.

Ed Garono's name would remain connected with Jaeckle right up to 1955, but long-time friend John Wick recalled that Garono dropped out of the picture when the "big merger" took place. As early as the 1920s, Garono was described as a "prominent corporate lawyer," a trustee of St. Louis Catholic Church on Main Street and then president of the church's Board of Trustees. Garono represented St. Louis Church trustees at a meeting in 1929 at which the pastor, Father Laudenbach, solicited legal advice on "how to avoid the appearance of consuming alcoholic beverages at social functions in the church." [6] Garono still was a trustee two decades later, well beyond our nation's experiment with prohibition. "He was a stern sort of fellow. Unlike Jaeckle, I never saw Garono smile," recalled Wick. [7]

A Shaky Political Start

Jaeckle's introduction to politics began while he was still in law school when a local tavern owner with his eye on a Republican State Committee seat enlisted young Jaeckle's support. It was Leo Schmidt who taught Jaeckle in this pre-women's suffrage era that Buffalo politics started and ended in the local taverns.

Schmidt and his young driver, Ed Jaeckle, boldly invaded a tavern used as enemy headquarters, and invited everybody to belly up for a free beer. There were glares all around but nobody accepted. Jaeckle, it was said, didn't take his first political deep breath until the pair made a hasty retreat to the street.

A week later, Schmidt and his young driver happened by the same tavern, walked in, and repeated the offer. After a long silence, a man at one table with three companions shouted out: "We'll drink with you Schmidt." They did and a few others joined in. The candidate didn't hang around long, and once outside, Jaeckle said: "Well Leo, we made some progress in there this time." "And why not?" was Schmidt's answer. "I planted those four guys." [8]

Jaeckle was to put Schmidt's tavern techniques to good use a few years later when at age 22, he was bucking the establishment and running for the nomination for ward supervisor. This time, when Jaeckle entered a tavern with just enough money in his pocket to cover the house, the proprietor angrily refused to serve the round. The bartender was a supporter of young Jaeckle's opponent and he wasn't about to let this upstart buy the drinks at his bar.

So day after day, Jaeckle stopped into the tavern, announced the drinks were on him, and sat there with his beer, working the crowd. Jaeckle confirmed years later that on his way out, he would tell everyone within shouting distance: "Sorry boys, I wanted to buy you a drink but this guy wouldn't let me." Jaeckle won that nomination and election and took his seat on the Board of Supervisors from the old 11th Ward in 1917. [9]

In addition to launching a political career that would take Jaeckle all over the country and would make "Jaeckle" a household name in the New York-Washington political establishment, the young supervisor developed one life-long habit and met his life-long partner during his first campaign.

As soon as he was elected, he got himself a driver, an idiosyncrasy that he would carry to his death. "Yes, he could drive a car," said his friend and colleague Ralph Halpern. "But he never did. A man of stature had his own driver."

More importantly, he met pretty Grace F. Drechsel, a neighbor and secretary for the manager of the Hotel Touraine, a fashionable Delaware Avenue hotel noted in 1902 for bathtubs and showers in every room. Grace helped Jaeckle with the phones and with typing during the 1916 supervisor race and accompanied him to all meetings, it is said, unless they were "strictly stag affairs." [10]

She continued working with him in his successful 1918 re-election campaign and they were married in 1920. Their family homes were only blocks apart in the Fruit Belt but there is no indication that they knew each other when they were growing up. Grace was a Catholic and likely would have attended St. Louis parish school instead of the local public school.

After their marriage, Grace preferred to remain in the background but she accompanied Jaeckle on political trips and stayed informed on political affairs. She enjoyed golfing, gardening and cooking and was known to compose poetry for her own and her husband's enjoyment. She would become active in Buffalo educational and cultural endeavors, including the former Rosary Hill College, the former Albright Art Gallery and the Buffalo Philharmonic, before her death on May 17, 1976. [11]

Jaeckle, working around a brief stint in the Navy at the end of World War I, won re-election to the Board of Supervisors in 1918, but he would not serve his second term. At the organizational meeting of that body in January of 1919, the supervisors named Jaeckle to the $3200-a-year job of board clerk, a position he held for seven years. As clerk, he was learning the political ropes and brushing shoulders with the city's political leaders. In addition, he had a stipend to help build his political structure, while leaving enough time to support himself through his legal practice.

The scrappy, brash young man with bright blue eyes and what was just becoming known as platinum blond hair was establishing a reputation as a reformer, and with that reputation came a guarantee of plenty of political enemies. His influence was increasing and in 1926 he managed to win a seat on the State Republican Committee from the 3rd Assembly District. With his new credentials, he challenged the local Republican leadership on its choice of candidates and was summarily ousted from the clerk's position in 1928. Not easily deterred, Jaeckle countered by running his own reform candidate for Erie County treasurer, an old friend from the Fruit Belt named Charlie Ulrich. Ulrich beat the mainline candidate and rewarded Ed Jaeckle with a political plum. Jaeckle became the county's collector of back taxes, a coveted political patronage position in which Jaeckle would received a portion of whatever back taxes his office was able to collect. [12]

For the next five years, both Democrats and some establishment Republicans tried every maneuver they could imagine to abolish Jaeckle's position, and in fact, Jaeckle himself was on record in favor of abolishment, an action he apparently didn't work very hard to bring about. But in each case, abolishment was blocked in Albany, where Jaeckle was beginning to make a name for himself. Once Gov. Alfred E. Smith blocked the action, calling it "blatant political retaliation," and a second time, it was blocked by Gov. Franklin D. Roosevelt, probably because Erie County's mainline Republicans favored abolishment. [13]

It was during this period – May 1, 1932 – that Jaeckle and Garono joined with Carlton E. Ladd and set up offices in the Rand Building. *The Buffalo Evening News* political reporter Jack Meddoff commented that the political reformer enjoyed "an extensive practice, Mr. Jaeckle's specialty being in the capacity of counselor in estate and financial matters." [14]

Local Republican leaders tried, usually unsuccessfully, to keep Jaeckle in line, and when questioned about it, Jaeckle told Meddoff: "I'm not against political organization. I am only against political leadership that places politics above the interests of the people and the party." Soon political organization would become the Jaeckle trademark.

The early days of the New Deal saw the local GOP struggling for its very survival and in a complex maneuver that would have made Machiavelli's cohorts proud, Jaeckle engineered a coup that saw Erie County Republican chairman Fred Bradley resign to seek a federal appointment he never received. By now, it was clear that young Jaeckle was a force to be reckoned with. Over the objection of the new Erie County chairman, Jaeckle won party nominations for his old friends, Leo Schmidt and Charles Ulrich. Then the new chairman, William J. Hickey, came under a blistering attack from Jaeckle and resigned to return to his first love, the judiciary and an open seat on the state Supreme Court bench. It was the Fall of 1935, the local GOP was in a shambles, its chairmanship was vacant, and Ed Jaeckle stood at the sidelines, ready to accept the call from his party to lead them forward, out of the political doldrums that had overtaken the once-proud local Republican Party.

In a front page story in the *Buffalo Times* on the day he accepted the county chairmanship, Jaeckle was quoted as saying: "I can assure all the members of the Republican Party that I shall conduct their affairs to the very best of my ability. I have no friends to reward and no enemies to punish." [15]

But in an inside story, the *Buffalo Times* could not help but to tweak the tail of the new GOP chairman, who they saw as a threat to local Democratic dominance and as a candidate championed by their competition, *The Buffalo*

Evening News: "Edwin F. Jaeckle swallowed his pride today. He accepted a job he swore and be damned he would never take, no matter if the Demmycrats overrun the countryside. Well, the 'Demmycrats' did, and Mr. Jaeckle changed his mind." [16]

Then after a reference to Jaeckle's stinging rejection as the GOP mayoral candidate in 1933, the *Times* quoted Jaeckle as saying: "Maybe I was too liberal. ... I believe that in liberal policies [lie] the future of Republicanism. ... We started out as a liberal party and I see no reason to change." This remark takes on all the more significance when you consider that conservatives Calvin Coolidge and Herbert Hoover had been his party's national standard bearers for a decade.

Jaeckle would hold the Erie County Republican leadership reins for the next 13 years, a period of rebirth for the local and state Republican organizations, but that would not occur until Ed Jaeckle and a group of reformers known as the "Young Turks" would lead a revolt that would shake the state GOP organization and drag it into the modern era.

But before that, Jaeckle ran into an immediate problem at home. No sooner had he assumed the local leadership role than he found himself without a viable candidate for mayor of Buffalo. Flush with success, he had his own name put on the November ballot in a five-way race that included a former mayor, another leading Democrat, a preacher, a so-called independent Republican, and Jaeckle.

On Nov. 3, 1937, Jaeckle came in second, losing to Thomas F. Holling by 1,427 votes in a contested election which would see Jaeckle call on the state attorney general's office to sort out the results. A page 3 *New York Times* story said Jaeckle had made "specific charges of alleged illegal voting and registration" in the Buffalo election. Although Jaeckle's letter to the governor was not made public, the *Times* said Jaeckle contended that "men at the Federal transient bureau had been illegally registered, that voters in several sections of the city had been 'colonized,' and that literacy certificates had been forged." [17]

After initially refusing, the courts eventually did order a recount which showed that Jaeckle remained No. 2 in the five-way race, and Holling was declared mayor of Buffalo. Jaeckle would never run for public office again and his sights now were clearly set on Albany and his role as kingmaker.

Taking on the State GOP

Just who was this Ed Jaeckle who had wrested control of the Erie County Republican Party and was making noises on the state level about the New York City-run "Old Guard?" According to Carl Wall, a *Buffalo Times* reporter given the task of profiling the new county GOP boss in 1935, Jaeckle was: "To the outward eye, a very pleasant fellow indeed. He looks more than his 41 years, but it is because of the solidity of his build and his prematurely gray hair. He has a most affable smile and an altogether easy manner. ... The kind of man who can drink champagne with bankers and beer with the boys in the back room." [18]

Shortly after assuming the Erie County chairmanship, Jaeckle began to put together a coalition of upstate chairmen and in 1936, he declared war on the "reactionary group" in control of the state Republican Party. He fearlessly attacked the leadership of Charles D. Hilles who had been the state's Republican National Committeeman for 24 years and had played a role in the Calvin Coolidge and Herbert Hoover elections. Jaeckle's second target was Republican State Chairman Melvin C. Eaton, whom he considered the puppet of the New York City Republicans.

The always straight-shooting Jaeckle didn't blindside Eaton. Nearly 40 years later, Jaeckle recalled that he walked up to the state chairman, who was quite full of himself, and asked him: "When are you going to retire?" Taken aback, the chairman assured Jaeckle there must be some mistake. "Well then, I thought you should know," said Jaeckle, "I'm going after you." [19]

This ensuing party fight was waged in full public view for eight months or more and the *New York Times* relished in daily stories about a crumbling New York State Republican Party. Jaeckle carefully chose his battleground, the New York State Assembly, one of the statewide patronage machines controlled by the Republicans. Two days after Christmas in 1935, the *New York Times* quoted Jaeckle at great length, denouncing the accepted practice of the Assembly speaker being chosen by New York City Republicans without even as much as a nod to their upstate colleagues. The *Times* said Jaeckle had not only crafted a coalition of Western New York chairmen, but had added the support of a rival faction in Suffolk County to challenge the leadership. [20]

What followed when the Assembly attempted to organize in 1936 was a blood-letting that would weaken the state GOP leadership and crack open the door for a wholesale change that would not be completed until after the next gubernatorial election in 1938. Jaeckle's coalition boycotted the Assembly reorganization meeting, leaving the GOP without enough votes to elect a speaker. Then in a series of back-room deals, including a handful of Democrats absenting themselves from the chamber for a crucial vote, a weakened Old Guard managed to elect its speaker, but not without concessions to the Jaeckle group. When the smoke had cleared, the *Times* declared that the rift had been healed with the "Erie leader and Assembly speaker entering a peace pact." Yet, Jaeckle was quoted as saying Erie County had been "vindicated," and "it must be obvious to all Republicans [that] Mr. Eaton has disqualified himself for the chairmanship of the State Committee." [21]

By April 1936, with the state leadership still officially in the hands of the Old Guard, The *New York Times* declared that the "Young Turks" had quietly taken control of the state party. And the leaders of the Young Turks were Ed Jaeckle and J. Russel Sprague of Nassau County. Jaeckle and Sprague, later joined by Herbert Brownell, were destined to control the state Republican Party, and then the National Republican Party, for the next 12 years, but at this point, they were names known only to insiders, appearing midway through a long Page One story in the *New York Times*. [22]

The state GOP leadership, as a sop to the Young Turks, named an upstate member of the Old Guard, William S. Murray of Utica, its new chairman, but within a month, a relentless Jaeckle was calling for his ouster, claiming Murray had "willfully deserted his post of duty" and was "guilty of gross neglect of official duty." [23]

Ed Jaeckle was playing hardball in the big leagues now. Two decades later, he would recall those years, saying: "Politics is a continual fight for decency against corruption and personal interest. You've got to do what's right or the public knows it. You don't fool anybody in this business." Then he added what would become one of his political pillars: "Politics is not cheap in itself; it's an honorable profession. But if you're in it for personal benefit or personal gain, your effectiveness is gone." [24]

When law colleague William I. Schapiro tried to recall Jaeckle's most striking characteristic, he said: "He was savvy. ... He knew human nature. Ed knew what made people tick. He was great at evaluating people, knowing their strengths and their weaknesses.... He wasn't fooled. Nobody could fool him.

He could see through everything." [25]

But despite those steely blue eyes that could peer right through you, Jaeckle was not perceived by his contemporaries as a stern man. Jovial and fun-loving but tough as nails were characteristics used by his friends. More than 50 years later, retired *Buffalo News* political reporter George Borrelli recalled this Jaeckle story:

"He had kind of a high-pitched, unusual, sort of nasal voice," said Borrelli. "When he was county chairman – I don't know if it is true or not but everybody believed it was – some job seeker went to his office to inquire about a patronage job he had sought. And Jaeckle supposedly said: 'You're my second choice for that job, pal.' Not knowing what to say next, the applicant asked: 'Would you mind telling me, sir, who your first choice is?' And Jaeckle, without missing a beat, is said to have answered: 'Anybody but you!'" [26]

By 1936, at age 42, Ed Jaeckle's influence had spread far beyond the Fruit Belt he still called home, and beyond his native city as well. He was a rock-solid liberal Republican in an age of New Deal Democrats and conservative Republicans. He was a back-room political brawler at a time when national politics was turning global and exceedingly gloomy. He no longer sought elective office for himself but he and his small group of close associates already had their sights on running New York State and, eventually, the nation. What they needed was a candidate they could crown king.

CHAPTER III

The Fleischmann Brothers: Designed for Success

If you grew up in the south end of the Village of Hamburg in the second or third decade of the 20th Century, you probably knew one of the six Fleischmann brothers. And if you befriended one of them, you befriended them all. Their large 2 - story frame house, built on a triple lot at 49 Central Ave. in a sleepy village 12 miles by train from Downtown Buffalo, was where neighborhood boys naturally headed on a mild late spring day. The Fleischmann place was the neighborhood playground.

When all the Fleischmann boys turned out for a pickup baseball game, they could make up the better part of a team on their own but they usually split up to make things fair. The side yard of the Fleischmann property, the side opposite the tennis court, was a baseball diamond when it wasn't serving as a winter toboggan slide. Edwin was the oldest, the biggest, and would remain the tallest of the brothers throughout life. He could hit the ball into the apple orchard at the end of the property for a ground rule double. And if there was any question about interpreting the rules, fourth son Manly would figure it all out and deliver a perfectly logical and well-reasoned verdict that invariably favored his team. In the midst of a good argument, you might hear a few "thees" and "thous" in a chorus that included mild curse words, but only by the brothers to each other, a little inside family signal of frayed nerves.

Even the youngest brother, Adelbert – named after a famous Buffalo lawyer and judge, Adelbert Moot – the shortest of the boys, eventually was able to smash the ball right out of the village, that is, right over the south property line into the field heading toward Water Valley and the Town of Eden. [1]

This was the young family of prominent Buffalo attorney Simon Fleischmann and his wife Laura. Simon was the first American-born son of a German immigrant, as was Ed Jaeckle's father, but that is where the comparison ends.

Grandfather Emanuel Fleischmann was born in Aufsess, a fertile valley in Bavaria in 1825 to a minor municipal court figure, the "hof jud," or the "Court Jew." Either to escape his family's leather and grain business or the defined fate of the youngest son, becoming a rabbi, or possibly just to fulfill his lifelong wanderlust, young Emanuel set sail for a new life in America in 1849. His odyssey would take him to New York City, then to Mississippi, New Orleans, the Isthmus of Panama, the Pacific Ocean and eventually San Francisco and the gold rush.

His quest for gold netted him barely enough to live, rather uncomfortably, but he eventually saved – and then lost – $42,000, a small fortune in those days, by making and selling cigars in the prosperous San Francisco of the 1850s. After a journey back to the homeland and a second harrowing Atlantic crossing to New York, a matchmaker and family friend from Bavaria arranged a marriage between Emanuel and Eliza Dessauer, and the couple settled in Iowa City just long enough for Emanuel to become a successful businessman and civic leader. But the lure of new-found oil and gas fields pulled the young family to Western Pennsylvania, and eventually to the growing metropolis of Buffalo, where he set up a cigar store on Seneca Street, taught Hebrew, played violin at music halls, taught music and held several teaching and administrative posts in Buffalo schools. [2]

His son, Simon Fleischmann, followed in the footsteps of his driven father. He was a precocious musician, an honor student, a law clerk for a young future president, Grover Cleveland, and eventually a prominent lawyer in the firm of Fleischmann, Pooley & Altman. The "Pooley" in the firm name was Maj. Gen. William R. Pooley, who would leave his Buffalo law practice behind for a distinguished Army career. Pooley led the 74th New York Infantry in the Mexican border campaign, and then in Europe during World War I, he participated in the Meuse-Argonne offensive and was named to head the Superior Provost Court in an area of occupied Germany. [3]

The one trait that Simon did not inherit from his father was the need to seek his fame and fortune in cities all over the globe, but some would say that the travel gene skipped a generation and turned up in full bloom in Emanuel's fourth grandson, Manly.

Simon however made his career and raised his family in the Buffalo area. He continued his parents' love for music and as a student is said to have ushered at the Academy Theater with his friend Bill Daniels, a founder of the downtown Buffalo music store, Denton, Cottier & Daniels.

A proficient lawyer, Simon was known for a caustic wit. He was a one-term member of the Board of Aldermen, representing a district that today is known as Allentown, and served as legal counselor to Mayor J. N. Adams. Despite his Jewish upbringing, Simon played the organ at Unitarian Universalist Church for many years. He was considered the premier organist at the Pan American Exposition and when Mayor Adams donated the famous exposition organ to the city for installation in the Elmwood Music Hall, Simon Fleischmann was given the official title of "honorary city organist." [4]

It was at the Unitarian Church that Simon met Laura Justice, a church member and a descendent of a Philadelphia Quaker family that traced its roots back to William the Conqueror and more recently to Philip Syng, the "Philadelphia silversmith who designed the silver ink well in which the signers of the Declaration of Independence dipped their quill pens." [5] Laura's father, William G. Justice, was city comptroller in 1910 and the family name was carried to the next generation in the couple's second son, Justice Fleischmann.

Simon had a home at 190 Edward St., just a few doors from Virginia Street, in a building shared with a tavern, and later a speakeasy. Although it is often repeated that Simon had this structure built, 190 Edward St. is mentioned as early as 1901 by Simon's father Emanuel, as the family home. [6] In any event, this was the city residence, a convenient location for Simon, within walking distance of the Buffalo Club where he took his meals when he stayed in the city. The club was founded in 1867 with Millard Fillmore as its first president, and Grover Cleveland as one of its later members. The friendships Simon nurtured there would play a role in the lives of future members Manly and Adelbert, as well as in the life of Ed Jaeckle, and many other deceased and current members of the Jaeckle Fleischmann firm.

Simon and Laura had the family's Hamburg home built near the end of the Buffalo & Lake Erie Tractions Line, a trolley that ran up Hawkins Street in Hamburg and had its northern terminus in Downtown Buffalo. Besides Edwin, Justice, Manly and Adelbert, the Fleischmanns had Dudley, the third son, and Lawrence, son No. 5, in a span of roughly 13 years. The Fleischmanns, while frugal, were said to have given their boys "books and music and broad fields to romp in," along with an inherent drive and the means to succeed: Everything from family contacts, the boys' print shop in the basement and an expectation that each would be an honor student and go on to college. [7] They even had their own music teacher in Simon's sister, Bianca, an accomplished organist who lived with the family in Hamburg.

Adelbert recalled the large dining room table in Hamburg, which on almost any Sunday held a huge pot roast, with vegetables and all the trimmings. Simon and Laura, the six boys and usually Aunt Bianca would be seated at the table and Simon would go "right around the line," expecting to hear each boy's best story or quip of the week. "You had to have a story or a joke, and you always wanted to top your brothers' stories," Adelbert said. [8] Simon had stories for the boys too. But it was said he saved his best lines for downtown, where he wouldn't be giving them away for free.

On religion, Adelbert said Simon agreed with his wife that the boys needed some religious education, but Simon claimed he didn't care whether it were Jewish or Quaker. "He knew damned well that there wasn't any Quaker church in Buffalo, so that made the choice very easy," Adelbert said. In a compromise, the boys attended temple at Temple Beth Zion downtown every second Saturday, and went to Sunday School most Sundays.

But on the question of using the Quaker idiom – the "thees" and the "thous" – at home, Adelbert pooh-poohed that as a myth that apparently was started in a 1952 major feature article in *Harper's Magazine* about his brother, Manly. They were brought up to refer to their parents as "thee," and that developed into an inside joke among the teenaged boys that you could justify mild cussing by dropping a "thee" or a "thou" into the sentence. "Of course, that was contrary to every tenet of the Quaker religion," Adelbert recalled with a chuckle. [9]

Manly: A Bumpy Road to Stardom

Manly, like his brothers, usually was at the top of his public school class without seeming to put much effort into his studies. But he did put effort into his saxophone. Born July 15, 1908, and named after his father's friend, Supreme Court Justice Manly Greene, Manly grew up at the height of the Jazz Age and he relished the music of his era. He put together a jazz and dance band he called Fleischmann's Hot Hamburgers to play around town. "That was Manly's contribution to the music world," brother Adelbert said with a laugh. "He was better as a lawyer." [10]

During his summers, he cut grass in Buffalo city parks, was a bellhop on Great Lakes passenger boats, clerked at a downtown hotel and was a farm hand in the Eden Valley. When he arrived at Harvard for his undergraduate work, he already had a reputation as a hell-raiser. By his junior year, despite a good academic record, he was on probation for the noisy parties he held in the dormitory. And somehow in the second semester of his junior year, Manly was expelled from Harvard.

Seventy-five years later, Manly's only child, Alison, cleared up the expulsion issue. She said her father, on a trip to Cambridge, pointed to a dormitory building and told his young daughter that he had come home from studying in the library to find his room cordoned off and police inside. "A security guard told dad that some crazy kid had been making bathtub gin from coconuts and the whole thing blew up," Alison recalled her father saying. "So daddy's Harvard career was over." [11]

Not about to go home in failure, Manly got a job as a ditch digger with a contractor friend in Dorchester to support himself while he set out to persuade Harvard authorities to readmit him. Later, he told a *Harper's Magazine* reporter that "My obvious desire to reform finally impressed the dean sufficiently to let me go to summer school and rejoin my class in September." [12]

After graduating from Harvard in 1929, Manly entered the UB Law School and again, he found his mind wandering from his studies. This time, he and his brother Dudley decided there was a pressing need for another advertising agency in Buffalo and they set up shop in an office on Main Street in Buffalo. This one-year venture was worth more in street smarts than in dollars. "We agreed to smoke a cigar every time we made a profit," Manly said. "We didn't smoke many cigars." [13]

So Manly returned to law school and graduated No. 2 in his law school class in 1933, and immediately began teaching international law and insurance law at the Law School and legal medicine at the UB Medical School. It is said that his work was so outstanding that he argued a case in the state Appellate Division the day after he was admitted to the bar.

The young lawyer gained a wide range of experience as the confidential law clerk for State Court of Appeals Judge Charles B. Sears, a friend of his father, and Manly would do considerable appeals work throughout his career. In fact, Judge Sears was one of Simon Fleischmann's three close friends who would play major roles in son Manly's life. Another was John Lord O'Brian, the famed Buffalo attorney and orator who was said to have put together one of the finest legal staffs in the country for President Roosevelt during World War II. And the third was Gen. William (Wild Bill) J. Donovan, the famous Buffalo general and trial lawyer who is credited with founding the Office of Strategic Service, better known as the OSS, the precursor to the modern CIA. [14]

In 1938, Manly Fleischmann took his only dip into politics. At age 30, he managed O'Brian's half-hearted losing campaign for the U.S. Senate. O'Brian's nomination had been orchestrated by Ed Jaeckle's forces at the New York State GOP nominating convention in Saratoga Springs, but there is no indication that the older Jaeckle and young Fleischmann knew each other at this time. They certainly would have heard of each other. O'Brian didn't even attend the convention which nominated him.

Fleischmann never showed strong political leanings. Besides managing the unsuccessful run by O'Brian, who ran as a Republican, Fleischmann worked for the Democratic Truman administration after World War II, he carried out several high-level assignments for New York's Republican governor, Nelson A. Rockefeller, and he generally referred to himself as a Democrat or an independent.

But back in the early '30s, Manly Fleischmann was a man on the move and was seen as an eligible bachelor. He was described as a slightly heavyset man of medium height, with a ruddy complexion, a curious abbreviated smile and a full head of wavy black hair. He could be serious, with flashes of youthful earnestness, and he could appear humorous and unharassed, enjoying a cigar and a glass of scotch whiskey. "Yes," acknowledged brother Adelbert, "he was what you might call a handsome man." Thekla Putnam, the widow of firm partner John G. Putnam Jr., gave it a woman's perspective: "Manly was a charmer. It was natural for him to be the center of attention in a very quiet and friendly way. You couldn't miss him even if he was standing quietly in the corner of a crowded room." [15]

In August of 1933, Manly married Lois Marseilles, who was reputed to be the prettiest in a family of four beautiful girls. Their father was a cellist for the WPA-era Buffalo Philharmonic Orchestra and the girls grew up in an Episcopalian household in a flat on Buffalo's West Side. The young Fleischmann couple, with their daughter Alison, who was born in 1937, was in constant motion, living in several homes in Buffalo, apartments in New York

City and homes in Arlington and Alexandria, Va.

The couple would celebrate their 50th wedding anniversary in 1983 with a dinner at the Buffalo Club, and would recall dinners at the White House and lunch at Buckingham Palace, conferences in cities all over the country, years in rented homes in Virginia, other years splitting their weeks between a home in Buffalo and one of several apartments in New York City. The occasional quiet fishing trips together broke up the excitement of Manly's breathtaking day-to-day pace. "Far be it from daddy to own a home and live in it for any time at all," recalled daughter Alison, reminiscent of her great-grandfather, Emanuel Fleischmann, whom she had never met. [16]

Adelbert: The Quiet Brother

When Adelbert was graduated from the Hamburg public schools, the last of the six Fleischmann brothers to go through the Hamburg system, it was expected that he would attend Harvard College like his brothers Edwin and Manly. But he had finished high school early and it was felt he was too young to go off to college on his own. So instead he spent a year in college preparatory work at the Nichols School in Buffalo.

Adelbert, born Nov. 20, 1912, was considered an avid reader in a family of readers. As a youth, he played the piano, but insisted later that "it didn't take." All the boys took lessons. "Because my aunt taught us, it was like taking medicine. 'Practice your piano. Practice your piano.' I can remember asking for one of my birthdays that I not be compelled to take lessons any longer. It was one of the biggest mistakes of my life. I wasn't half bad. I just hated to practice." [17]

Adelbert entered the UB Arts College and majored in literature as an undergraduate, before going off to Harvard Law School where he earned his law degree. Adelbert and Manly were not only brothers, they were best pals as youngsters and closest friends throughout their lives. So upon being admitted to the bar, Adelbert joined with brothers Justice and Manly in a law firm they called the Fleischmann Brothers. It is said the firm's name took some good-natured ribbing from downtown colleagues because, as Manly put it, "it sounded like a firm of green grocers." [18]

But before long, war in Europe was in the air and most young men's thoughts were on eventual U.S. involvement in an overseas war instead of building careers at home. Adelbert Fleischmann, while at Nichols, had befriended

Owen B. Augspurger Jr., the son of a successful Buffalo businessman. Although Augspurger went off to undergraduate school at Princeton University, and then returned to Buffalo to take his law degree at UB while Adelbert was at Harvard, the two remained friends throughout their college years.

And then with war impending and the prospects of the draft likely, Adelbert and Augspurger decided to join the National Guard at the old West Delavan Avenue Armory. Describing himself as "an original draft dodger," Adelbert explained that the Guard unit had been a cavalry unit but had been recently converted into an anti-aircraft unit and it needed educated recruits for this new and tricky assignment. [19]

So the two young lawyers and friends from Nichols joined, pledging to attend summer camp and serve a year on active duty. But as fate would have it, during that year, the European war came to the U.S. and the safe haven of the National Guard unit was converted into the 102nd Anti-Aircraft Battalion and shipped off to Australia.

Owen Augspurger and Adelbert Fleischmann would serve side by side throughout World War II, bonding a friendship that would last until Augspurger's unexpected and tragic death 25 years later. The pair would serve together in Australia, New Guinea and the Philippines, where their anti-aircraft guns were used primarily to protect Allied supply depots from Japanese air attack. Adelbert recounted his biggest surprise of the war: While we were on leave in Australia, Owen fell in love with an Australian girl named Paula Norris; he married her during the war and eventually brought her back to Buffalo after 1945.

By V-J Day, Augspurger was commanding officer of the 102nd Battalion, and upon his return to the U.S., he was succeeded in that position by Adelbert Fleischmann. [20] In typical Adelbert fashion, he summed up his military career 60 years later this way: "The Japs heard I was in Australia. The word must've got out. So they never came near us." [21]

Manly and the War

Manly Fleischmann's wartime service sent him in a much different direction from that of his younger brother, a direction that would open doors and widen channels for the young attorney and law school teacher. John Lord O'Brian was named general counsel of President Roosevelt's Office of Production

Management and then the War Production Board. Both the office and the board were tools created by the Roosevelt Administration, first to supply the weapons for America's allies in Europe, and then to manage supplies during this country's all-out war effort. O'Brian called on young Fleischmann, along with some other young Buffalo lawyers, to join him in Washington. Manly would become his assistant general counsel and the leader of what some newspapers began to refer to as O'Brian's Buffalo Herd. Among them was James O. Moore, who in later years would become a judge back in Buffalo. O'Brian knew Manley Fleischmann not only through the 1938 Senate campaign. His relationship with the Fleischmanns went all the way back to his visits to Simon Fleischmann's home when Manly was a boy. So in 1940, Fleischmann, with his wife and three-year-old daughter, moved to their first Washington area residence at 2239 North Quincy Street in Arlington, Va.

After Pearl Harbor, the restless Fleischmann mounted an effort to get out from under his stateside desk job. He sought a Navy commission but was rejected because he was overweight. Alison was a child but she recalls her father getting up at dawn every morning, putting on his sweatshirt and pants and lumbering down to the Potomac River and back, a distance of about a mile and a half, in an attempt to sneak under the Navy's officer weight limit. [22]   He eventually gained his commission and as a Navy lieutenant, he was loaned to another of his father's friends, Gen. William Donovan, and was dispatched to Lord Mountbatten's Indian Ocean Theater. Fleischmann was an operations officer in Ceylon and then on Ramree Island off Burma, where he directed a 100-man espionage unit behind the Japanese lines in Burma and Thailand. This duty would earn Manly Fleischmann a bronze star and a Presidential Unit Citation, and commendations from the government of Thailand, which still was called Siam at that time. [23]

It should come as no surprise that Manly's favorite movie was "Bridge On The River Kwai," the only film he could sit still through, according to daughter Alison. And yes, years later, he did see "The King and I," on Broadway, with Yul Brynner playing the enlightened king of Siam.

After the Japanese surrender, the Navy loaned Fleischmann to the State Department, where he was general counsel to the foreign liquidation commissioner during negotiations of international settlements involving the Lend Lease program. Manly told friends that this assignment, which he expected to

be brief, was his way of hitching a plane ride back to the States, instead of waiting his turn for an uncomfortable troop ship crossing of the Pacific. But
throughout this period, Manly was gaining invaluable government contacts and
experience, working with some of the top legal minds of his generation. This
government exposure would play a major role in his post-war life.

1945: Putting Life Back Together

For millions of war veterans across the nation, V-J Day was a time of relief,
a time of celebration, and a time to start piecing together a life and career with
family and friends that had been so far away for five years. No other generation of Americans had ever faced such a daunting task. The Japanese attack on
Pearl Harbor had acted like a film placed on permanent hold for millions of
careers, families and lovers. And now it was time to flip the switch and continue
the film from where it had left off, a task that proved difficult for many and
impossible for some. Adelbert Fleischmann, with his feet always firmly planted
on solid earth, was ready for the challenge. His first order of business was to
marry his sweetheart from Boston, Helen Lois White, whom he had met at
Ft. Edwards, Mass., before he was shipped to the Pacific. Like hundreds of
thousands of others, this couple didn't have time for a formal wedding in their
hometown. "I was discharged in El Paso, Texas," Adelbert recalled, "and Helen
came down from Boston by train...and we got married. We couldn't wait."
Sixty years later, he still enjoyed teasing that he met Helen in a Boston bar, a
story that held a grain of truth and contained a lot of good-natured stretching.
From El Paso, the newlyweds went by train to St. Petersburg, Fla., to visit
Adelbert's mother, and then, on their way to Buffalo, they spent several days in
Washington with Manly. The couple arrived in Buffalo on Nov. 12, 1945, and
made their home in a flat on Ashland Avenue. On his first day back in town,
Adelbert located an office in the Ellicott Square Building suitable to set up a
practice of law. [24]

Two days later, he was on the phone to his old friend Owen Augspurger who
said he had two old desks stored away and would offer them as his initial contribution to the new practice. So on Nov. 14, 1945, both men went back to
work. By the fall of 1946, they were joined by Manly, who upon completing
his post-war assignment had moved his young family back to Buffalo into a flat
on Richmond Avenue. A third brother, Justice, briefly joined the new law firm

of Fleischmann & Augspurger with offices in Ellicott Square. [25]

By Oct. 20, 1946, when veteran reporter H. Katherine Smith profiled the three returning war veterans in the Sunday *Courier-Express*, it appeared that life for the Fleischmann brothers finally was about to return to normal. Or was it? Could it ever be the same, especially for Manly who had been so close to the source of power in a nation that had been thrust into a new position of leader of the free world.

But before we can continue moving forward, we must stop and drop back to pick up the story of Ed Jaeckle, whose life had taken quite a different set of twists during the years the younger Fleischmann brothers were fighting a war in the Pacific.

CHAPTER IV

Jaeckle:
Ten Years in the National Spotlight

When Thomas E. Dewey made the trip to Saratoga Springs for the New York State Republican Convention on Sept. 29, 1938, this fashionable little town where New York City's wealthy and would-be wealthy summered already was beginning to show its rough edges. It still boasted its white colonnade resort spots like the Grand Central Hotel whose guest list included the likes of the Vanderbilts, the Whitneys, the Rockefellers and J.P. Morgan, but ten years of the Great Depression were taking its toll on this hamlet 189 miles up the Hudson from New York City.

Republicans from all over the state had gathered at the Saratoga Convention Hall to hear the acceptance speech of a gubernatorial candidate who might challenge the New York City Democratic machine's stranglehold on the state. Ed Jaeckle, at 44 the leader of a group of liberal Republican reformers, and already gaining a reputation for his smooth-talk bullying tactics, had put together an upstate-downstate coalition for Dewey, the young New York City district attorney who had been making headlines as the squeaky-clean government reformer and gangbuster.

Newspaper reports made it clear that the entrenched old guard GOP, including Robert Moses, Kenneth Simpson and Bully Hill were not enamored with the way Jaeckle had slammed together a "New York City-Erie County steam roller," but their resentment did not carry over to candidate Dewey, and besides, the Old Guard had been in turmoil since 1934 when Moses lost the state by more than 1 million votes. [1]

Dewey, always a stickler for precise timing, entered the packed convention hall to a standing ovation at exactly 7:15 PM, 15 minutes before the National Broadcasting Company was to go on the air with his speech. When he climbed the steps to the convention hall stage, accompanied by former U.S. Attorney George Z. Medalie, and amidst the cheers of the delegates, he was introduced for the first time to Erie County Chairman Edwin F. Jaeckle, the man most responsible for his nomination. That simple introduction and handshake would kick off a rough-and-tumble political relationship that would reshape the national Republican Party.

In direct contrast to the impeccable Dewey, Jaeckle was described as "spectacularly unphotogenic, a hawk-nosed, jowly figure, gruff of voice and manner, blunt, ambitious, not yet 45, but a grizzled veteran of Republican wars in Buffalo." [2]

Dewey's speech, which contained the usual rhetoric of those out of power and the usual calls for the party faithful to pull together and oust those in power, was pre-empted by NBC after 14 minutes for an announcement from Munich that a four-power agreement on Czechoslovakia had averted war in Europe. The world was safe. Hitler had promised to halt his aggression.

Buffalo Evening News political reporter Jack Meddoff wrote ten years later that this convention marked the political discovery of Dewey as someone beyond a crusading New York County DA, and he credited Jaeckle with the "discovery" that would catapult both men into the national spotlight. This characterization was picked up and embellished over the next 35 years and at Jaeckle's death in 1992, the New York Times put its stamp of authenticity on the statement, adding that Jaeckle had said of the discovery: "I was not Dewey's man, nor was he mine. Events brought us together. We were a very strong combination. ... I was like a trainer with a good horse." [3]

An indication of the state of the Republican organization that Jaeckle and Dewey would inherit could be seen in reports that the men were patching together the rest of the statewide ticket at the convention hall and in their suite in the Grand Central Hotel hours later. Jaeckle was on the phone to Rochester, trying to determine the correct spelling of the name of Julius Rothstein, who had been chosen for state comptroller, and John Lord O'Brian of Buffalo, who was given the U.S. Senate slot on the ticket, told reporters that he was surprised to learn of his nomination over breakfast the next morning in the Knoxville, Tenn., newspaper.

In the general election, Dewey lost to the immensely popular incumbent Gov. Herbert H. Lehman, whom the Democrats enticed to seek re-election against his wishes for fear of losing the state to the upstart Republican reformers. But the slim loss rejuvenated the state Republican Party and did little to slow down the efforts of Dewey and the man from Erie County who already was being referred to in the always sensational New York City tabloid press as "Buffalo's Mahatma." As a footnote, the Dewey ticket carried the formerly Democratic stronghold of Erie County by 35,000 votes, and in the final days of the campaign, when Jaeckle was turning out 1000 faithful Dewey supporters at a wet pre-dawn Buffalo rail yard rally, an apprehensive Gov. Lehman sought and received the public support and endorsement of a fellow New Yorker, President Franklin D. Roosevelt.

The so-called Young Turks of the party led by Jaeckle spent the rest of 1938 and early 1939 consolidating their hold on the state party, and beginning to build a viable political organization, styled after what Jaeckle had built in Erie County. Within three weeks of the election loss, the *New York Times* reported that Jaeckle, "who fought against New York City control of his party for two years," would be Dewey's choice for chairman of a new Republican State Executive Committee, which was seen as a way around the conservative, Old Guard Utica chemist, William S. Murray, whose party chairmanship would continue into 1940 and who refused to step aside before his term was up. Two years was too long for Dewey and Jaeckle to wait.

In January 1939, at a dinner in Albany, Dewey cut a deal for Jaeckle to take over control of the state party. Murray would keep his title and the $12,000-a-year salary that went with it, but Jaeckle would take over the power of the chairmanship. In return, Jaeckle would sign a personal note to cover the state committee's $40,000 outstanding debt. And almost immediately, Jaeckle, never one to be shy about asking for money, got word to the Wall Street fund-raisers that it was their job to raise funds for the party, and it was his job to allocate them. [4]

When Jaeckle was officially elected state GOP chairman a year later, Dewey already had set his sights on the White House, occupied by FDR, and had pulled together three men who for the decade of the '40s would be known as Dewey's Triumvirate: Jaeckle, close associates J. Russel Sprague and Herbert Brownell. The three would have various titles over the next eight years, but one or another of them always would be in charge.

And as a sign that Jaeckle was a man to be reckoned with, Alf M. Landon, the titular leader of the national Republican Party's liberal wing, wired Jaeckle:

"Dear Ed: I am delighted at your unanimous election as Republican State Chairman of New York because you will make a whale of a good chairman in a very critical campaign and because of your early association with the liberal crowd in the Republican party.... Heartiest congratulations and best regards." [5]

Jaeckle had been an early supporter of Landon in his unsuccessful run against Roosevelt in 1936 and was seen as an important factor in continued friendly relations between the Landon and Dewey factions.

To understand Ed Jaeckle in his mid-life and at the height of his political power, one must take a closer look at Dewey, the racket buster and the nemesis of the New York mob, who became universally known as the man on the wedding cake, and the "only man who could strut while sitting down." [6]

In so many respects, Jaeckle and Dewey were opposite poles of a magnet, but in other more subtle ways, their views on government were so strikingly similar that for the rest of their lives, one would be hard-pressed to distinguish which of them had originally coined some of their common political axioms.

Dewey, who became known as the proprietor of Dapplemere Farm at Quaker Hill, an exclusive mountain community 64 miles north of Times Square, strove to maintain the image of the educated country squire who carried on his business life in Manhattan. But in fact, he was the precocious son of a backwater Michigan newspaper editor and was brought up in Owosso, Mich., near Lansing. He aspired to sing on the stage of the Metropolitan Opera – or at least Broadway – and after excelling at Michigan State, he put aside his hopes of vocal stardom and headed to a job at a New York law firm. He never looked back to Michigan.

As New York County district attorney, he was his own star prosecutor, and made headlines chasing New York gangsters, racketeers, extortionists and prostitution lords. He convicted big names like Waxey Gordon and Lucky Luciano and missed out on the famed Dutch Schultz only because Schultz's gangland enemies got to him first. Dewey's crime busting made him a star of the New York media, and according to Dewey's definitive biographer, Richard Norton Smith, 55 million moviegoers saw pictures of the gangbuster in weekly black and white newsreels. When a woman from Brooklyn called Fred Allen's radio show to predict a Dodgers pennant, Allen was said to have quipped that if the team won two more games that season, Dewey would investigate them. At New York's Inner Circle dinner, which satirized the city's political establishment, Dewey was portrayed as "Diogenes Dewey" in search of an honest man.

Dewey himself went to great lengths to project the image of an upscale New Yorker, as opposed to Jaeckle, who is described numerous times as "a flashy dresser who uses a mule-skinner's language."   Jaeckle never carried on any pretensions. You saw exactly what you got in Jaeckle. Whereas Dewey went as far as to try to get the editors of the *Saturday Evening Post* to change a reference to his Saturday night poker games to Saturday evening bridge parties. [7]

Yet Dewey was a candidate of the 20th Century, an opponent of Old Guard conservative Republicans, and a candidate who preferred radio addresses to whistle stops, and finely tuned speeches to pressing the flesh. Jaeckle usually is credited with teaching Dewey how to shake hands and kiss babies, but even late in his campaigns for the presidency, long after he had mastered the art of shaking thousands of hands, his method was described as mechanical.   It was Ed Jaeckle who would spot a familiar political crony in a crowd at a whistle stop, and leave the train to give his old friend a sincere handshake and hug.

Yet, philosophically, the two were not so far apart. Dewey was known to quote Thomas Jefferson: "The whole art of government consists of being honest."   Jaeckle's colleagues heard that quote in all its various permutations over the decades.   One of Dewey's often quoted maxims was that no man should be in public office who can't make more money in private life. [8] Jaeckle refused all offers for political patronage jobs during a decade which saw him almost continuously on the campaign trail and seldom at home, yet newspapers would go on describing him as a well-off Buffalo attorney.

Dewey expressed an ambition early on, according to biographer Smith, to get out of politics and head a big New York law firm and get rich. Jaeckle retired from politics to do just that and he accomplished his goal.

 Dewey cut his political teeth in a city where organization was everything. Political clubs chose party officers and convention delegates, designated preferred candidates for primaries and reproduced themselves through captains, assembly district slates and propaganda. Jaeckle was the consummate political organizer and proved it over and over in Buffalo, Erie County, New York State and then on the floor of two national conventions.

And finally Dewey was an administrator who demanded absolute loyalty to his person. Jaeckle was a political leader who demanded absolute loyalty to the party organization. And both were their own men. It was only a matter of time before these two giant personalities who were so dissimilar yet so much alike would rub together, creating heat and then flame.

In 1939, with similar ambitions, the two men appeared to be walking in lock-step. No sooner had Jaeckle wrested the state party chairmanship from the Old Guard in April, than rumors of a Dewey run for the Republican nomination for president began to surface in New York City. One must understand that in 1939, when New York City had three of the 16 major league baseball teams playing within its boroughs, and the westernmost major league ball clubs played within sight of the Mississippi River in St. Louis, New York State had about one in every ten voters in the nation. A solid New York State party rep-resented the largest bloc of voting delegates at a national political convention.

But a solid New York State Republican Party proved hard to come by. A front page headline in the *New York Times* on April 13, 1940, reported: "Dewey in Control of State Machine; Jaeckle Chairman," followed by a drop that read: "Move to Oust Simpson from the National Committee Opens Bitter Debate." The story went on to detail a rift in the state party between those new to power and those reluctant to give it up. Threatening to put up a roadblock to any Dewey presidential nomination were Kenneth F. Simpson of New York County, the state's national GOP committeeman, Southern Tier powerhouse Bully Hill, and a Rochester right-wing Republican newspaper publisher, Frank Gannett, who was seeking favorite son status for himself. Gannett would become the founder of the powerful Gannett Media organization, which would change the shape of American newspapers in the second half of the century with the launch of *USA Today*. [9]

Dewey was not without his own upstate newspaper support. In Buffalo, Ed Jaeckle's close friend, Alfred H. Kirchhofer, with the backing of Edward H. Butler Jr., the owner of *The Buffalo Evening News*, would be in constant con-tact with Dewey through three campaigns for the White House. And as Jaeckle Fleischmann partner Randy Odza pointed out in an interview a half century later, it was common knowledge that Jaeckle and Kirchhofer spoke with a single voice.

As early as June 2, 1939, Kirchhofer was writing Dewey: "I spent several hours yesterday with Gov. [Alf] Landon [of Kansas] and Ed Jaeckle discussing matters in which you have an interest." Kirchhofer then goes on to urge Dewey to mend his fences with Simpson and to put Jaeckle in charge of an organiza-tion to seek the presidential nomination. [10]

That mending never did take place and at the sweltering June 1940 Republican convention in Philadelphia, Jaeckle, the New York State Republican chairman and the man designated by Dewey to handle the convention floor, had to fight for his convention credentials because the state's credentials had been presented to Simpson. Even so, Jaeckle brought a drum and bugle corps to Philadelphia from Buffalo's East Side, the Uncle Sams, to play for convention delegates in the hallway and eventually, he did gain admittance to the floor.

On the day of the nominating vote, neither Dewey nor Robert Taft of Ohio could muster enough votes to win the nomination and gaining strength was a compromise candidate named Wendell Willkie. With Jaeckle and Russ Sprague working the floor, Willkie began to pull ahead, and Jaeckle set out to craft a compromise with the Taft floor manager. But on the sixth ballot, Kenneth Simpson got his revenge. He called for a poll of the huge New York delegation, which split between Dewey and Willkie and the split spelled the end for a Dewey nomination. [11]

In a *Buffalo Evening News* story, written in advance of the 1948 convention, political reporter Meddoff dispelled 1940 with two sentences: "Mr. Dewey and Mr. Taft killed each other off in that memorable 1940 convention and the virtually unknown Wendell Willkie became the nominee." Four months later, in one of his "Dear Kirk" letters to editor Kirchhofer, Dewey lauded Jaeckle, saying "I … think he did a perfect job in handling the Convention." [12]

According to biographer Smith, Jaeckle, always a realist, had recognized early on that a Dewey election that year was not in the cards. [13] Roosevelt would be near unbeatable in 1940. The Nazis were advancing all over Western Europe and Dewey, not yet 40 years old, had no international experience. But always looking long, Jaeckle had urged that the candidacy go forward as a springboard for the future. By the time Wendell Willkie was being thrashed at the polls in November of 1940, the Battle of Britain and an inevitable American involvement in another European war were stealing the headlines across the nation.

Winning the Executive Mansion

When Kenneth Simpson died unexpectedly a few months later, and with Willkie relegated to the bone heap of one-shot wonders, Dewey and the

Triumvirate set their sights on the New York executive mansion in Albany. Gov. Lehman had been a reluctant candidate in 1938 and he pledged not to seek re-election in 1942, leaving the door wide open for a new governor. Jaeckle had fashioned a state party controlled by discipline and strength at the top. No doubt, the party would control the 1942 state convention scheduled for Jaeckle's hometown, Buffalo. But, when it became apparent that Wendell Willkie, in one last show of strength, might oppose Dewey for the nomination for governor, Jaeckle pulled the plug on the Buffalo convention, where it might have become difficult to control the delegates on the floor, plus 13,000 spectators. He moved the convention back to Saratoga Springs and a hall just large enough to hold the delegates, the hall where he had met Dewey four years earlier. [14]

The party faithful, under Jaeckle's watchful eye, nominated Dewey for governor without opposition, and on Nov. 3, 1942, Dewey was elected governor over a colorless Democrat named John J. Bennett by 647,000 votes. The former DA came within a whisker of winning Manhattan County, a feat unimaginable four years earlier. While Jaeckle, Brownell and Sprague were savoring the easy Dewey sweep, the New York press was postulating on the prospects of Dewey heading up the national ticket in 1944.

In fact, the day after the election, editor Kirchhofer mailed a "Dear Tom" letter from his newspaper office at Main and Seneca streets in Buffalo, congratulating the new governor and alluding to the White House. But further down in the letter, Kirchhofer chided the former prosecutor, possibly on the advice of Ed Jaeckle, reminding him that newspaper reporters and photographers were "not in the witness box." Then he said: "You have a bad name with the reporters and I don't believe you want that to be so. They now can be helpful."

With the 1944 national press corps obviously in mind, Kirchhofer said: "If you want to go higher, as we hope may eventuate, they are indispensable." The editor closed his letter with this apology: "Please excuse my frankness, but I think somebody must say this while there is time to plan to face the music." [15]

It is no wonder Jaeckle and Kirchhofer were such close friends. They both grew up on Buffalo's German-American East Side, they both were fearless, blunt and truthful to a fault, and they both wanted to see a Republican in the White House above all else.

For the first year of the new state administration, it was Jaeckle's job to whip the State Legislature into shape. During the session, he lived in the Ten Eyck

Hotel in Albany. At the time, Albany was a city of 130,000, and 5000 of them were government employees. Buffalo, the 14th largest city in the nation, boasted a population of 576,000. Dewey had wanted to run the state from Dapplemere Farm in Pawling instead of moving his family to the creaky executive mansion in out-of-the-way Albany, but Jaeckle and Brownell convinced him that would tarnish his image. In a compromise move, Jaeckle worked out a sweetheart deal with the management of the Hotel Roosevelt in Manhattan for Dewey to take over two floors of the hotel for his New York City offices. Two decades later, Nelson Rockefeller would maintain a state executive suite in Manhattan but he didn't need to work out any deals with hotel owners for Midtown office space.

In May 1943, the *New York Times* ran a story claiming that Jaeckle was running the State Legislature and often speaking for the governor. The *Times* recounted how the Triumvirate took part in weekly Sunday Night War Councils at the Roosevelt at which Dewey and legislative leaders decided what actions would be taken in the legislature. Once agreed, they always were enacted. Jaeckle saw to that. [16]

One of those actions was recalled in 1964 by Buffalonian Frank C. Moore at a testimonial dinner for Jaeckle in the Buffalo Club. Moore recounted how Jaeckle reminded the governor in 1942 that an obscure state board set up for the study of malignant diseases had not met in 14 years. On Jaeckle's urging, Dewey replaced the membership of the board with Buffalo's Kirchhofer and four distinguished doctors, who within four years transformed the 1897 Gratwick cancer research laboratory founded by Dr. Roswell Park and *Buffalo News* owner Edward H. Butler into what would become the world renowned cancer research center, Roswell Park Memorial Institute, and later, the Roswell Park Cancer Institute. The institute with ties to UB and Buffalo General Hospital where Dr. Park was surgeon in chief, is within a mile of Jaeckle's ancestral home on Buffalo's East Side. [17]

It is during this period, with Jaeckle spending so much of his time in Albany or on the road for Dewey, that the often-told story of Jaeckle's turning down a state patronage job occurred. Jaeckle told *Buffalo News* reporter Anthony Cardinale in 1980 that Dewey had said: "We haven't talked about your appointment. You're the first person. What do you want?" Jaeckle said he later was offered the secretary of state position at $12,000 a year, plus a car, chauffeur and expenses. "I don't want anything," was Jaeckle's response.

"I can't understand why you don't want anything," Dewey said. Running the State Legislature is "going to cost you some money."

Jaeckle recalled that his response was: "That's all right. I can afford to carry on. I want to be free." Jaeckle said he explained that he wanted to be leader of the party, and wanted to cooperate with the governor, but that he didn't want any commitments. [18]

At another time, Jaeckle told his friend and law partner William Schapiro about what was slowly becoming a love-hate relationship. "I got the idea from Ed that Dewey never understood or quite trusted Ed," Schapiro said, adding that Jaeckle insisted that Dewey suspected he was on the take somewhere. It drove Dewey nuts that he couldn't find it. "Here he was, the great prosecutor and he couldn't find anything," Jaeckle would tell his colleagues years later, always ending the story with: "…because there was nothing to find." [19]

The '44 run for the Presidency

By late 1943, Dewey was showing all the signs of a presidential candidate, while insisting publicly that he wasn't running for anything. Jaeckle, Brownell and Sprague were given the task of winning over the Midwest that had stopped him cold in 1940. Biographer Smith speculates that Dewey did have a certain ambivalence about 1944. [20] President Roosevelt had already made it clear that he was not going to campaign in any traditional way. He didn't need to. The aging President was seen daily in newspapers and in weekly newsreels with Winston Churchill, Josef Stalin or Gen. Dwight Eisenhower as the Allies plotted how they would retake Europe and crush Nazi Germany. But Dewey knew he couldn't turn his back on the Republican Party and maintain any chance to gain the nomination in 1948, when presumably the war would be over and Roosevelt would step aside, leaving wide the door to the White House.

On Dec. 9, 1943, editor Kirchhofer sent a "Dear Governor" letter, opening with the revelation that he "had a long talk with Ed Jaeckle last night." He then went on to discuss pre-convention strategy, saying that the war-time transportation director's suggestion that both conventions be held in Chicago was a good one. Kirchhofer added: "Mr. Willkie doesn't want to meet there and that seems another good reason for going to Chicago." Kirchhofer than warned against an attack on the Roosevelt administration's foreign policies and the carrying out of the war, citing perceived errors but opining that "altogether too many people with sons in service likely feel" that politics should stop at the ocean's edge. Two days later, Dewey wrote a "Dear Kirk" letter, expressing similar concerns and assuring him that these matters were being discussed with Sprague and Jaeckle. [21]

Dewey was still playing a cat and mouse game with the press over his candidacy in May 1944 when *Time Magazine*, in an issue featuring a picture of Charles De Gaulle on the cover, called Dewey a presumptive presidential candidate and quoted Chicago bookmakers giving 4 to 1 odds on a Dewey nomination. More importantly, *Time* revealed that Dewey had put together an election task force "unequaled since the first Roosevelt Brain Trust," and led by Russ Sprague, Ed Jaeckle and Herb Brownell. They described Jaeckle as a "bulky, well-heeled Buffalo lawyer, who almost single handedly turned Buffalo's meager Democratic majorities into Republican landslides." There was no question the Triumvirate had hit the big time. And in keeping with the media's penchant for erroneous predictions, *Time* predicted that if Dewey received the nomination, he would install either Sprague or Jaeckle as Republican national chairman.[22]

As the June convention opened, the *Washington Post* speculated on a Dewey nomination by acclamation. Jaeckle had been cast in his usual pre-convention role of working the political leaders and favorite son candidates. Ohio's Robert Taft was neutralized by being named the convention's permanent chairman. Illinois's Everett Dirksen withdrew, as did California's Earl Warren. By the opening of the convention, the only remaining serious candidates, Gov. John W. Bricker of Ohio and Harold E. Stassen of Minnesota, were privately conceding that there was no stopping Dewey. And then Bricker dropped out in return for the vice presidential nomination. Now, the *Washington Post* predicted that Herb Brownell would be named national GOP chairman, but conceded that Jaeckle or Sprague could get the nod. By the time Dewey's name was put forth for nomination on June 29, there was no need to vote. That evening, Thomas E. Dewey stood before 25,000 cheering Republicans in Chicago Stadium and accepted their nomination, without a floor fight. [23]   And syndicated political columnist Marquis Childs concluded that now Dewey has just four months to "perform a miracle."

What should have been a triumph of political organization of the highest magnitude for Ed Jaeckle was short-lived. One day later, the story broke that Herb Brownell would become chairman of the Republican National Committee and would direct Dewey's campaign. Jaeckle insisted he had urged Dewey to choose Brownell and the *New York Times* explained that Jaeckle was needed to concentrate on New York's 47 electoral votes, but neither was very convincing. [24] Historian Smith said that in choosing Brownell over Jaeckle, the candidate "bruised the feelings of Ed Jaeckle, a mistake that was to have huge ramifications." [25]

Then in a second slight within a month, Jaeckle, seeing the need for a dramatic stoke, conceived a plan to have Dewey visit the troops at European battlefields, with possible face-to-face meetings with Churchill and Stalin. According to biographer Smith, Dewey's immediate reaction was: "God, that's a marvelous idea" but urged Jaeckle to keep it to himself so that it could be sprung at a time of maximum exposure. However within days, at a strategy meeting in Albany, in front of an expanded inner circle, Dewey dismissed the idea out of hand with the comment: "We're not going to do it," and moved on without further discussion. In a characteristic reaction, Jaeckle said years later that he recalled answering: "Then you can run your own campaign." [26]

Jaeckle's later-years partner back in Buffalo, Odza, said he had heard that story over the years and that Ed Jaeckle had thought Dewey had a shot at beating President Roosevelt against all odds. "You've got to do something to show your connection to the troops, the people, your human side has to be there," Odza quoted Jaeckle as saying. "If you don't, you're going to get clobbered." When Dewey squelched the idea with a wave of the hand, according to Odza, that "really cemented Jaeckle's thought process that Dewey was not willing to do what had to be done to become President of the United States." [27]

By all accounts, Dewey waged a hard but uninspiring campaign. He attacked Roosevelt's War Production Board in a major Philadelphia speech, leading editor Kirchhofer to remark that the material was "way over the heads of most Americans." And before 93,000 cheering partisans in Los Angeles, Dewey delivered a speech on unemployment insurance and Social Security with all the detail and precision of a master prosecutor. Even Brownell remarked afterwards: "They didn't get it!" But in all fairness, it must be pointed out that just weeks before the nominating convention, the largest invasion in the history of the Western Civilization had been launched on the beaches of

Normandy, and as the presidential campaign wore on, with little participation by the incumbent President, some of the most legendary battles of World War II were playing out daily on the front pages of every newspaper in the nation. And there was no doubt in the American psyche that FDR was their commander in chief.

At the end of the day on Nov. 7, 1944, President Roosevelt won 36 of 48 states (Alaska and Hawaii had not yet attained statehood), and took 432 of the 531 votes in the Electoral College. The Republicans cited the popular vote to call it the closest presidential race since 1916, but by today's standards, the winner was never in question. Dewey lost his own New York State by 316,000 votes. And FDR won all the major upstate cities, including Jaeckle's Buffalo. Thirty-five years later, Jack Meddoff, by then the retired political reporter for *The Buffalo Evening News*, told colleague Anthony Cardinale that Jaeckle told him Dewey would no longer take his advice "in preference to that of Herb Brownell or Russ Sprague because they meekly submitted to Dewey's opinion and views, whereas Jaeckle would forcefully present his own views." [28] Some said often too forcefully.

A half century later, Erma Hallett Jaeckle, Ed's second wife, recalled Jaeckle saying that "Dewey kind of turned against the people who were responsible for getting him where he was. But Edwin didn't dwell on that. He was a very affirmative thinker, but he was conscious of it." [29]

In any event, 10 days after the election, Jaeckle's smiling picture was in the *New York Times*, next to the bombshell headline: "Jaeckle Quits Post in a Surprise Move." Jaeckle had resigned his position as New York State Republican chairman, apparently without telling Dewey, Sprague or Brownell. According to the *Times*, Jaeckle had issued a two-sentence statement that read: "I hereby tender my resignation as chairman of the New York State Republican Committee. This resignation is to take effect immediately." He brushed off *Times* questions about differences with Sprague and Brownell, claiming he wanted to devote more time to his law practice in Buffalo. [30]

1948: Another Run and another Disappointment

What followed was a temporary hiatus from the national spotlight for the Triumvirate, and especially for Jaeckle, who continued on as Erie County Republican chairman, a post he had held since 1935, but he was not an active participant in the state committee or in the Dewey campaign for re-election to the executive mansion.

The death of President Roosevelt in April 1945, after he had served only a few months of his unprecedented fourth term, changed the dynamics of the national political scene. No longer would the field be wide open for a new president in 1948. Harry S. Truman would be running as an incumbent, having served just a few months shy of a complete term. And it would be a convulsive term at that. In quick succession, the war ended in Europe, Truman ordered the dropping of the first atomic bombs, Japan surrendered in the Pacific, labor strife developed at home with unions attempting to gain ground lost in wartime, and the crush of returning servicemen to the work force and the housing market all but overwhelmed an otherwise relieved nation. To add to the convulsive nature of the years immediately after the war, inflation was mounting, and what had been perceived as a Soviet threat in Europe had quickly developed into the Cold War. School children were learning to hide under their desks and cover their eyes to protect themselves from Soviet nuclear weapons.

At home, Gov. Dewey was moving ahead with plans for a four-lane divided highway from New York City to Buffalo and beyond. With no stop lights over its entire length, it would shave nine hours from the New York-Buffalo motor trip. Dewey projected it would cost $202 million and Democrats called it "Dewey's Folly," reminiscent of "Clinton's Ditch," and following a similar route to that taken by Gov. DeWitt Clinton more than a century earlier. Gov. Clinton, it might be noted, later suffered a narrow loss to James Madison in his bid for the White House.

In 1946, Gov. Dewey was re-elected to a second term by just short of the 60-40 margin generally considered a landslide. Then somewhere in the summer of 1947, when back in Buffalo the last of the electric streetcars were disappearing from Bailey and Kensington avenues in favor of new, rounded-edge buses, the Triumvirate was back together, meeting in Albany. The *New York Times* later would explain only that the 1944 "breach has since been healed, but it is notable that the first step toward reconciliation was taken by Mr. Dewey, not Mr. Jaeckle." [31] That same *Times* article showed how Dewey had greatly expanded his inner circle to include Elliott V. Bell, state superintendent of banking, as his chief speechwriter, Paul E. Lockwood, the governor's secretary, as operations chief, James C. Hagerty, in charge of press relations, and Paul E. Talbott, director of fund raising. John Foster Dulles and his brother Allen W. Dulles were placed in charge of policy. Quite a stable for a reluctant office-seeker. Some called it a full-court press.

Three decades later, Jaeckle would only say of his reconciliation with Dewey that the governor had pulled him aside during a fancy house party in Albany and told his former confidant that he was considering another run for the White House, but that he would only undertake the task if Jaeckle would rejoin him. It was an open secret in *The Buffalo Evening News* newsroom by the late 1950s that editor Kirchhofer had initiated the reconciliation. And in 1980, with Kirchhofer and Jaeckle still quite alive and able to refute the story if they chose, *News* reporter Cardinale wrote that "without telling Mr. Jaeckle about it, Mr. Kirchhofer traveled to Albany, where he found Mr. Dewey in bed with a heavy cold. He told the governor that Mr. Jaeckle – if he were approached the right way – could be persuaded to take an active role in the campaign. ... Soon they were back together." What would Jaeckle get in return? News reporter Meddoff in February of 1948 asked Jaeckle just that question. His response: "I make no commitments to others and I don't expect anyone to make commitments to me." [32]

Despite the reconciliation, Jaeckle's policy role clearly had been diminished. In the late summer of 1947, Jaeckle was calling in political favors in the South, glad-handing old friends and winning pledges of their delegates. Jaeckle was clearly in the middle of a February 1948 war council to plan Dewey's entry into primaries, a phenomenon that was just beginning to take away from the smoky backroom caucuses of the national conventions. His layoff hadn't dulled his political eyesight. Jaeckle urged Dewey to skip the Wisconsin primary, considering that Harold Stassen, a young Joe McCarthy and Gen. Douglas MacArthur all had their sights on that state's early primary. Jaeckle was overruled, and the result was: Stassen – 19 delegates; MacArthur – 8 delegates, and Dewey – 0 delegates. [33]

But by convention time in June 1948, the Dewey house was back in order and everything was under control. Dewey's convention headquarters in Philadelphia's Bellevue-Stratford Hotel had all the organizational trademarks of Ed Jaeckle, including individual index cards on every working delegate to the convention. Every state delegation had a Dewey liaison to report back on every action. Dewey workers distributed cold soft drinks to the steamy delegates and their families while other Dewey workers distributed Dewey favors and Dewey door prizes, along with the usual buttons. Herb Brownell was in charge of the convention floor. *Time Magazine* profiled the Dewey convention team, detailing how every member had a specific duty to carry out. In charge of "practical politics and the panzer divisions" were familiar names: Jaeckle, Brownell and Sprague. The entire convention had been orchestrated like a fine symphony. After the first ballot, Dewey had a wide lead over Taft, Stassen, Gov. Earl Warren of California and a handful of favorite sons. After the second ballot, with Dewey still 33 delegates short of the nomination, Jaeckle was seen on the floor, giving the governor of Connecticut some firm but friendly advice. The third ballot was a mere formality, resulting in the unanimous nomination of Thomas E. Dewey. Earl Warren, who released his delegates to the Dewey camp at a key moment, would be the vice presidential nominee. [34] Nobody in the orchestra missed a beat.

By September, the *Washington Post*, characterizing speculation over the Dewey cabinet in the upcoming administration as "the most overwritten story of the presidential campaign," wrote that Jaeckle, Sprague and Brownell, "could undoubtedly have any post that they wished" in the next administration. [35] Years later, Jaeckle insisted back in Buffalo that he wouldn't take part in such speculation with Dewey and at one point even told the candidate not to waste his time speculating; he hadn't won the prize yet. Jaeckle claimed that had led to an outburst from Dewey like nothing else he had ever seen. [36]

Jaeckle would later downplay his role in the 1948 campaign. But while he carried no official title, he clearly was part of the fateful decision early on to take the high road, refrain from playing in the gutter, from attacking President Truman and from threatening a fragile peace around the world. [37] With Dewey ahead by as much as 20 points in the polls, there seemed to be no need to upset the applecart.

Jaeckle rode the 17-car railroad train named the Victory Special as it crisscrossed the nation at least twice. It had cars for reporters, who it was said could leave their dirty laundry and have it picked up clean at a stop the next morning. There was a suite for the speechwriters, headed by Bell, a suite for the staff, a suite for Dewey and his wife, Frances, and often his mother. Food was prepared on the train. And of course, it contained the obligatory rear platform. It was said that at one stop, the ever-punctual candidate finished his speech before the train was ready to leave the station, and Ed Jaeckle had to block the door to discourage Dewey from turning his back on a cheering crowd.

But despite all the organization, the confidence and the polls, it was not to be. Journalists and political historians have speculated for decades over how Dewey could have squandered such a lead and lost the White House to Truman. Maybe it was overconfidence. Maybe it was a failed experiment in running a civil and intelligent American presidential campaign on the issues – just what the pundits claim the public desires. Maybe Dewey came across as just a little less than human. But none of those answers take into full account the residual effect on a tired nation of the Great Depression, World War II, and by his death, the idolization in some circles of President Roosevelt. Nor do they consider the inexplicable attraction of mid-America to the scrappy underdog president who the public urged on with the familiar "Give 'em hell Harry," or Truman's street-brawling toughness, honed under the tutelage of the Pendergast machine in Missouri.

Years later, Jaeckle was not averse to telling battle stories about this election to enthralled colleagues around a table at the Buffalo Club, the Lafayette Hotel or the Executive Club atop the M&T Bank Building. He was quoted universally as counseling Dewey to counterattack as only prosecutor Dewey knew how, while Truman kept up his barrage of constant and sometimes desperate attacks. "I told him that as a former DA he should attack," *Buffalo News* reporter George Borrelli wrote in a column quoting Jaeckle in 1974. "That he couldn't be a milquetoast and expect to win the election. But he believed the polls. He didn't want to rock the boat." Yet Dewey's secretary told biographer Smith that in the final weeks of the campaign, when Dewey insiders began to worry about a noted shift in public opinion, a livid Dewey wanted to blast Truman. According to Lillian Rosse, who claimed to be in attendance at the meeting aboard the Victory Special, Hagerty, Lockwood, Dewey's wife Frances, and finally Ed Jaeckle all urged the candidate not to give up the high road approach. [38]

Law colleague Bill Schapiro recalls Jaeckle recounting the well-publicized train engineer incident when a tired and frustrated Dewey publicly berated the railroad engineer outside the Victory Special for abruptly backing and then braking the train. Photos and newspaper accounts of the incident appeared throughout the nation. "Ed thought that was such a political mistake," Schapiro recalled. "To pick on a poor working guy … and to have the press and the country see it. What a big, big mistake, Ed would say." [39]

Another colleague and partner, Ralph Halpern, recalled Jaeckle saying: If Dewey had any charisma at all, he would have won, adding: "If Tom had listened to me, he would have been President." And there was colleague Paul Weaver's favorite Jaeckle observation: "If he only would have shaved that mustache, he'd have won." [40]

Dewey did finally take the gloves off with less than 100 hours left in the campaign, following Truman's reference to elite East Coast Communist sympathizers, but it was way too little and way too late. When the Dewey inner circle, including Jaeckle, gathered in the Hotel Roosevelt victory suite, to digest the returns early on Nov. 3, 1948, the man who had been ridiculed by prominent journalist Clare Booth Luce as "the little chap who looks like a bridegroom on a wedding cake" had swept the Northeast but the incumbent Truman had won the election by 2 million votes and by a count of 303 to 189 in the Electoral College. Surprisingly in Jaeckle's Buffalo and Erie County, Dewey had made a better showing against Roosevelt in '44 than he did against Truman in '48. [41]

After the election, Dewey went on to become a young elder statesman. He would serve another term as governor and would play a role in the nomination and election of Gen. Dwight D. Eisenhower in 1952. Jaeckle, still only 54 years old, would retire from politics for good, throwing all his energy, his savvy, his experience and his countless contacts into his Buffalo law practice. And despite their differences, Jaeckle, right into his 90s, would tell anyone who would listen that he still thought Dewey would have made a fine president. It had been quite a decade from that meeting on stage at the Saratoga Convention Hall in 1938.

* * *

As a postscript to the Dewey years, partner and colleague Odza tells this story, dating from the late 1960s. Historian Richard Norton Smith had gone to Buffalo and taped several interviews with Jaeckle in preparation for the writing of his 700-page biography, *Thomas E. Dewey and his Times.* Jaeckle had insisted as a pre-condition that he receive copies of the interview tapes. And now, under the guise of being interested in the Buffalo law firm's new billing system, Dewey had contacted Jaeckle about a planned visit to Buffalo.

"Understand, I never did trust Tom Dewey," Jaeckle told Odza in prefacing the story. "I wanted to make sure I had copies of whatever I said about him. And I told it straight. ... I didn't believe for a minute Tom was coming here about our billing system. I knew exactly why Tom was coming here."

Odza picks up the story told to him by Jaeckle only days or weeks after the Dewey visit:

"According to Jaeckle, Dewey came and sat down across the desk from Ed and started talking about the law firm. And then he got around to it. 'Ed, weren't you interviewed for a biography?' Jaeckle's answer: 'Yeah.' 'Were there tapes?' asked Dewey. Jaeckle's answer: 'Yeah.' 'Well, could I have them?' asked Dewey. 'No,' Jaeckle said, without changing his expression. And then pointing to his right-hand lower desk drawer, he added without raising his voice, 'That's exactly where they're going to stay.'" [42]

CHAPTER V

Manly Fleischmann:
A Star on the National Stage

"A big shot?" Alison Fleischmann repeated the question as she pondered what life had been like in Washington a half century earlier, for the only daughter of the man the press was calling the third-most important person in Washington, behind President Harry S. Truman and his secretary of state.

"The school I went to, everybody's father was a big shot. The chairman of the joint chiefs of staff's kids were on my school bus. Senators called every night. A limo might pull up to take daddy to the White House. So that's just the way it was." [1]

Following World War II, Manly Fleischmann had spent some time in Arlington, Va., and White Plains, N.Y., and then nearly five years establishing a law practice in Downtown Buffalo with his brother Adelbert and associates Owen Augspurger, John Henderson and Dwight Campbell. The practice was solid but not overly lucrative.

Then in September 1951, Fleischmann got a call from Washington. The West was enmeshed in a struggle with Soviet Communism for the domination of Europe and it had been 15 months since the Democratic People's Republic of Korea had lobbed mortars at its neighbor across the 38th parallel, thrusting the Korean peninsula into war between East and West. That forgotten war, fought in a faraway finger of land hanging from the Asian continent, has been described by some historians as the great test of the resolve of the democratic West and the communist East Bloc. It would end in a stalemate between the superpowers that would continue until the fall of the Berlin Wall in 1989.

Manly Fleischmann had co-authored with John Lord O'Brian the procedures for controlling production during World War II, so it was natural he would be called upon to serve as general counsel to Truman's national production board. The *Buffalo Courier-Express* speculated that the job would carry with it a salary of between $10,000 and $15,000 a year. [2] Within months, Fleischmann was named administrator of the National Production Authority. In a press release sent to *The Buffalo Evening News* on Jan. 24, 1951, Secretary of Commerce Charles Sawyer made the announcement, pointing to Fleischmann's work during World War II. It is curious that in the biographical portion of the news release, the portion normally written by the subject himself, Manly is described as a lecturer on international law at the University of Buffalo and the former president of the Buffalo Council on World Affairs. [3]

It also was noted that back in Buffalo, Fleischmann had engineered a turnaround of the bankrupt Sterling Engine Co. A federal judge in Buffalo had placed Sterling in receivership and Manly had been appointed receiver. When he stepped in, Sterling was said to have been down to its last $3,000 in cash assets. Two and a half years later, under Fleischmann's stewardship, Sterling had cash assets exceeding $1 million. [4]

During his two years with the Truman administration – two years that kept him at the center of constant controversy – Fleischmann was known by several bureaucratic titles, but in the end, he held the dual titles of administrator of the National Production Authority and administrator of the Defense Production Administration.

It is difficult to understand how two government bureaucratic positions with bulky titles could be equated with the third most important position in the administration unless one recalls that our nation was in the midst of the post-World War II recovery. Millions of families, deprived for more than 15 years stretching back to the Great Depression, wanted new homes and all the material goods they considered their just bounty. Labor strife had cut into a fast-growing economy. Workers often had more money in their pockets than stores had goods to spend it on. And now the President was saying: Hold on. We need to produce tanks and weapons and munitions, as well as new cars and refrigerators. Truman called this his policy of Guns and Butter. And the person who would make it happen would descend into a no-win boiling caldron. He would have to be a man of steel nerves, a man of the highest integrity and a man who had no political aspirations. That was Manly Fleischmann.

According to *Harper's Magazine*, the two agencies headed by Fleischmann had to devise production schedules and allocate scarce materials, issue priorities and control the use of production plants. It was his job to see that the nation maintained a flow of weapons to the armed forces and materials to the atomic energy program, while somehow diverting enough to civilian use to prevent a disruption of the economy. *Harper's* said that means "Fleischmann is the man whose decisions determine how many television and radio sets will be built next month and next year. He decides … how much steel Detroit may have for passenger cars, how much rubber Akron may have for tires." [5]

Manly knew the spot he had been thrust into and was quick to defend it. Upon being sworn in to his dual roles by Supreme Court Justice Tom Clark, Fleischmann said: "Almost everyone is aware of the fact that the free nations of the world are engaged in a bitter struggle for survival. … Any relaxation which prevents us from meeting rearmament goals now would merely give the Communists the chance 'to move again, where they will, when they will and how they will.'" [6]

Put in those terms, it is easier to understand that the pressure of conflicting interests on Fleischmann was overwhelming. He once said it was like "always living at the bottom of the ocean." [7] Work days of 12 to 14 hours were insufficient to even allow him to catch up with the latest problems so he said he operated on the principle of "selective neglect."

Time Magazine was one of Fleischmann's big detractors, scoffing when his ban on "frivolous construction" was extended to bars, cocktail lounges, golf courses, swimming pools, tennis courts and yacht basins. [8] In May 1951, *Time* complained that cuts were being made in steel for cars, television sets and stoves and that producers of durable goods were being told to get by with 20 percent less steel than they had used the year before. And when corporate leaders chided that Fleischmann was butting into everybody's business, Manly, already a mass of frenetic activity, retorted that he didn't have time for that. "[Commerce] Secretary Sawyer says he wants to see me daily. Mr. Wilson [Truman's mobilization czar] says he wants to see me daily. And Congress will probably want to see me daily. I won't have any trouble keeping busy." [9]

It is during this time that daughter Alison recalls attending a pajama party with her classmates from St. Agnes Episcopal School for Girls at the home of Georgia Black, whose father Hugo was a Supreme Court justice. The Blacks lived around the corner from the Fleischmann home at 212 Prince St. in Alexandria, Va. The Fleischmann home had been a hotel in the Revolutionary War era and it was believed Gen. Washington stayed there, across the street from the home of his personal physician. Anyway, Mrs. Black received a call

from her husband during the pajama party that he was bringing home some colleagues to work into the night. That sent the 13-year-old girls squealing and
scurrying to clean up their popcorn and Coca Cola bottles.

"We were supposed to clean up and get upstairs before Mister [Justice] Black
arrived, but the line of limos with their flashing lights started pulling up in front
of the house before we were finished," Alison recalled. "It was becoming obvious that some big shot was coming over with the justices. As we ran for cover
upstairs, President Truman came into the house and immediately invited us to
stay for just a little bit. He sat down at the piano, and in those days, Patti Page's
'Tennessee Waltz' was the rage. The President said: 'Here's something you'll
all recognize' and he played it on the piano. Then he said 'I've got another
favorite,' and he played the Missouri Waltz for us. For 13-year-old girls, it can't
get much better than that." [10]

At age 43, Manly Fleischmann was seen as one of the ablest administrators
in Washington. He made it clear he had no political ambitions and that his
intention was to return home to Buffalo and his law practice when the task at
hand was completed. His judgment was unfettered by political loyalties and his
decisions were unhampered by past ties to business, labor or other big interests. [11]
Even so, it took a fast wit to dissipate the tension in a room full of disgruntled
corporate executives. One day, standing before a group of gloomy looking
executives, Fleischmann began in a soft tone: "Well gentlemen, the CMP is a
howling success," referring to his new Controlled Materials Plan. The executives weren't impressed so Fleischmann added: "The consumer thinks it's a
success and the steel industry is howling." After what was described as an
explosion of laughter, everyone got down to business.

One of the highlights of his Washington years was the time in the Fall of
1952 when he and his wife Lois flew to the West Coast for a speech. Lois hated
to fly so they planned a cross-country train ride back to Washington. But a call
from the White House changed that and Manly flew back to Washington on his
own. The occasion was a meeting of the Cabinet with Winston Churchill.
Fleischmann found an empty chair in the back row of the cabinet room and
Winston Churchill came in with Anthony Eden and President Truman.
Churchill quipped that this time, the Brits had come "not for aid but for trade."
He praised the nation's program designed to supply the free world with
weapons while keeping the economy going at home. He praised the author of

the plan and asked if Manly Fleischmann was in the room. To applause from the cabinet, Truman called Manly to the head table where the men shook hands all around.

Later in the day, Secretary of State Dean Acheson held a quiet party for his British guests, and Churchill and Fleischmann had a long chat about defense production. "And mother missed that too," said Alison. "She was on a train somewhere out west." [12]

However this meeting led to a return visit to London in 1957, this time with Lois Fleischmann. The invitation read: "The Lord Chamberlain is commanded by Her Majesty to invite Mr. and Mrs. Manly Fleischmann to an afternoon reception in the garden at Buckingham Palace." [13] There is no record of how that reception went except Lois would recall meeting Queen Elizabeth in her backyard. In a scrapbook containing the Queen's invitation is another invitation, this one from Bess Truman, inviting Lois Fleischmann to lunch at the White House.

EⅡR

The Lord Chamberlain is commanded by Her Majesty to invite

Mr and Mrs Manly Fleischmann

to an Afternoon Reception in the Garden of Buckingham Palace on Monday 29th July 1957, from 3.30 to 5.30 o'clock p.m. (Weather Permitting) Morning Dress or Lounge Suit.

The invitation to Manly and Lois Fleischmann to meet Queen Elizabeth II in the garden of Buckingham Palace in 1957. Manly had discussed Cold War production with Winston Churchill.

Courtesy Alison Fleischmann

On May 8, 1952, the *Washington Post* reported that with his NPA and the DPA work completed and in place, Manly Fleischmann would resign his government positions and return to his private law practice in Buffalo by the end of the summer. The *Post* reported that "against heavy pressure, he prevented a repetition of the ineffective and inflated priority system of the early [War Production Board], and succeeded in the prompt creation of the Controlled Materials Plan as a substitute." [14]

His trip home was postponed when Truman sent Fleischmann to Paris as part of the American team to renegotiate reparations under the guise of the North Atlantic Treaty Organization. And then as Truman was preparing to leave office, the President offered Fleischmann the ambassadorship to Indonesia, but this time, Manly Fleischmann turned down the President's offer and instead returned to Buffalo.

A few years later, Manly recalled walking through the lobby of New York's Waldorf Astoria and seeing the former president waiting in line to check in. He walked up and asked Truman if he didn't want to jump to the front of the line but Truman let Manly know what he thought of any ex-president who couldn't wait his turn.

"Truman had a bit of a split personality," Manly Fleischmann told *Buffalo News* reporter Anthony Cardinale in 1979. "On the one hand he was a small town Missouri politician. On the other hand, he had a great sense of history and was acutely conscious that he had become president by accident. In my book, he was one of the great presidents." [15]

Manly Fleischmann: In Another Thankless Job

It would be 17 years later, and the stage would be New York State rather than Washington, but it seems appropriate at this point to go out of sequence and follow Manly Fleischmann to his next encounter with the spotlight of public opinion.

Law partner Randy Odza recalled that the year was 1969. A few lawyers were sitting around, discussing a case in the Liberty Bank Bldg. offices when Manly Fleischmann joined the group. Soon the discussion turned to a telephone conversation Manly had just had with New York's Gov. Nelson Rockefeller. Odza, then a young Cornell graduate only recently hired by the firm, remembers Fleischmann saying the governor had just characterized public education – particularly its funding in New York State – as a mess. The governor added that he was setting up a major commission to study the question and to recommend fixes. Rockefeller wanted Fleischmann to chair the commission.

"Why me?" Fleischmann told his colleagues he asked Rockefeller. "What the hell do I know about education? I'm just a lawyer from Buffalo." It was the country bumpkin routine, Odza said 35 years later, and a savvy Rockefeller didn't buy it. It was precisely because he was not an educator and not politically active that Rockefeller had chosen him. Even before he accepted the job, Fleischmann's fear was that a great deal of time and effort would be invested in a report that would end up gathering dust in someone's file cabinet. [16]

On Oct. 28, 1969, within a few days of that conversation in the Liberty Bank Building offices of Jaeckle, Fleischmann, Kelly, Swart & Augspurger, the governor, with typical Rockefeller fanfare, announced the formation of the new commission to conduct "one of the most penetrating studies of education ever made in this state." He introduced the commission chairman, Manly Fleischmann, at a posh Syracuse reception, describing him as "a trustee of the state university and a wartime defense production administrator." He named that panel of 16 experts the New York State Temporary Commission on Quality, Cost and Financing of Elementary and Secondary Education. That unwieldy title rankled Fleischmann right from the start, but the press, and then the government, almost immediately referred to the blue-ribbon panel as the Fleischmann Commission. [17]

This was not the first task Fleischmann had undertaken for Rockefeller. In 1963, concerned about widespread corruption in the administration of the state's arcane Alcoholic Beverage Control Law, Rockefeller appointed Fleischmann to a three-member panel to try to straighten out that mess. But after 15 months of study and six major recommendations, the so-called Moreland study was diluted by the State Legislature because it offended the Council of Churches and the state's package store owners. [18]

The education study would be different. Rocky had assured him of that. Fleischmann was splitting his time between New York and Buffalo during this period because of his affiliation with Webster, Sheffield, Fleischmann, Hitchcock & Chrystie in New York. He had taken upon himself the burden of actually writing the report and according to partner William Schapiro, it "took an enormous amount of his time for three years." Daughter Alison recalls that

he worked at the commission office on Second Avenue, five blocks from the
Jaeckle Fleischmann apartment at Second Avenue and 47th Street. [19]

On Jan. 29, 1972, the *New York Times* announced on Page One that the
Fleischmann Commission would recommend that "the state take over the raising and distributing of all non-Federal funds for public schools" and that to pay
the bill, the state would levy a uniform state property tax to replace local school
taxes. The *Times* said the commission would call for a freeze on school spending by the wealthier districts and massive spending programs for disadvantaged
students. It was noted that school funding programs, which relied primarily on
real estate taxes in the locality in which the public school was located, already
had been declared discriminatory and unconstitutional in California, Texas,
Minnesota and New Jersey, and that the Fleischmann proposal was seen as a
way to legalize New York school spending. [20]

Within a month, a second volume of the report was out, calling for 54 districts in the state, including New York City, to be compelled to bring about
racial balance in their schools, "using busing of pupils as a tool where necessary." It also called for an end of state school aid to parochial and private
schools. [21]

Time Magazine, in its February 7 issue, said that after more than two years
and $1 million in research, "lawyer Manly Fleischmann, a registered independ-
ent," argued strongly that poor schools must be brought up to the level of rich
ones. *Time* paraphrased the commission in explaining why the local property
tax did not work, using the examples of blue-collar Levittown and the North
Shore town of Locust Valley. But the example could just as well have been the
City of Buffalo and the Amherst Central School District. After explaining the
commission's state taxing scheme, *Time* said the rub was that "rich towns
would be forbidden to raise more money by imposing additional taxes on themselves." [22]

As might have been predicted, a massive firestorm of protest rose from several
quarters. Suburban school boards immediately cried foul. Yet, the New York
City budget director said: "Any commission that imposes extra burdens on the
City of New York for the benefit of well-off suburbs cannot be serious." Even
the usually supportive *Buffalo Evening News* ran first a cautious editorial under
the headline "Fleischmann Plan Too Extreme," and then followed it with another
editorial that praised the report but concluded:

Edwin F. Jaeckle retired
from politics at age 54
after gaining national
prominence in the
Republican Party. Once
he retired from politics
to devote full time to
his law practice, he left
politics behind.

Jaeckle Fleischmann Archives

This 1917 Jaeckle photo appeared on a
campaign poster. Jaeckle was seeking
re-election to a seat on the old County
Board of Supervisors.

Jaeckle Fleischmann Archives

Presidential candidate Thomas E. Dewey,
center, accepts the Republican nomination
at the 1948 GOP National Convention in
Philadelphia. With him are Jaeckle, right,
and House Speaker Joseph W. Martin Jr. who
was instrumental in Dewey's nomination.
Despite the polls and a famous Chicago
Tribune erroneous headline, Dewey lost
to Harry S. Truman.

Jaeckle Fleischmann Archives

State GOP Chairman Ed Jaeckle
gavels the 1942 state convention
to order at Saratoga Springs in the
same hall where Jaeckle first met
Tom Dewey in 1938

Buffalo News Archives

An already prematurely gray Ed Jaeckle
takes part in a radio broadcast at WBEN
studios in the late 1930s.

Jaeckle Fleischmann Archives

Ed Jaeckle entertains presidential candidate Dewey and his wife, Frances, during a campaign stop in 1944. Frances had sung bit roles on Broadway and Dewey once aspired to sing on the Metropolitan Opera stage.

Buffalo News Archives

Alf M. Landon, the leader of the progressive wing of the National Republican Party, chats with Jaeckle in 1942. Jaeckle had been an early supporter of Landon who lost to Roosevelt in 1936.

Buffalo News Archives

The 1948 Republican team to retake the White House included, from left, Herb Brownell, Paul Lockwood, Ed Jaeckle, California Gov. Earl Warren, Presidential candidate Tom Dewey, Sen. Bill Knowland and Russ Sprague.

Buffalo News Archives

New York Gov. Nelson Rockefeller chats with Jaeckle in 1960. Rockefeller sought Jaeckle's advice on key state questions during the 1960s and early 1970s.

Buffalo News Archives

Joseph Swart joined the Jaeckle firm in 1953 when Jaeckle was in the Rand Building. Later, he helped reclaim an American Airlines plane seized by the U.S. government in Buffalo.

Courtesy Michael Swart

Harry J. Kelly was first associated with Jaeckle in 1935. Kelly litigated two early aviation cases involving the old Bell Aircraft Co.

Courtesy Monsignor James Kelly

Edward J. Garono and Jaeckle were in practice together as early as 1916.

Jaeckle Fleischmann Archives

Manly Fleischmann, circa
1955, at the offices of
Fleischmann, Stokes &
Hitchcock in New York City.
Fleischmann commuted weekly
between New York and Buffalo
for nearly 25 years.

Courtesy Alison Fleischmann

Navy Lt.(jg) Manly Fleischmann directed an
espionage unit behind Japanese lines in Burma
and Thailand during World War II.

Courtesy Alison Fleischmann

Manly and brother, Adelbert, aboard the RMS
Queen Elizabeth in 1969.

Courtesy Alison Fleischmann

Albert R. Mugel joined the
Fleischmanns in 1954. He
continued teaching at the
UB Law School until his
death in 2003.

Jaeckle Fleischmann Archives

Adelbert Fleischmann still
maintained an office in the
Jaeckle Fleischmann offices
at 12 Fountain Plaza in 2007,
at age 94.

Jaeckle Fleischmann Archives

Owen B. Augspurger Jr.,
a tireless civic leader and
schoolboy friend of Adelbert
Fleischmann, died in a horse-
riding accident in 1969.

Buffalo News Archives

The Fleischmann brothers at the family home in Hamburg were, from left, Edwin, Justice, Dudley,
Manly, Lawrence and Adelbert.

Courtesy Alison Fleischmann

U.S. Secretary of Commerce Charles Sawyer congratulates Manly Fleischmann upon his swearing in as administrator of the National Production Administration in 1951. A proud Lois Fleischmann looks on.

Courtesy Alison Fleischmann

Manly Fleischmann with his catch while vacationing in Mexico, circa 1968.

Courtesy Alison Fleischmann

Manly borrowed daughter Alison's fir hood to keep warm during a 1967 fishing trip to Labrador.

Courtesy Alison Fleischmann

Members of the Jaeckle Fleischmann executive committee in the summer of 2007 were, top from left, Joseph P. Kubarek, Randall M. Odza and Mitchell J. Banas, and seated, Dennis P. Harkawik, left, and Edward G. Piwowarczyk, chairman and managing partner.

Jaeckle Fleischmann photo

Founding partners Ed Jaeckle, left, and Albert Mugel open the Batavia satellite office in 1981 at 10 Ellicott St., Batavia. The office served special needs in the Genesee County area.

Jaeckle Fleischmann Archives

"In our view, the Fleischmann cure for [school district] inequities went need-lessly far toward a totally egalitarian statewide standard of equal-dollars-per-student. ... This would forbid even a minimum supplementary enrichment effort by live-wire communities committed to educational excellence." [23]

The United Federation of Teachers went further, condemning the Fleischmann Commission report as serving "no useful function" and "paving the way for the destruction of the New York City public school system." [24]

In a *Buffalo News* commentary by Jerry Allan, the dean of Albany newspaper correspondents, he said the report, a blue, 1500-page, three-volume work pub-lished by Viking Press, "issued with wide publicity in January cluttered up offices in Albany. 'It's nice to put on a chair,' a secretary said, 'when I have to reach something from the top shelf.'" Allan continued that there was very lit-tle quarrel with the Fleischmann philosophy in Albany, but that the report nonetheless would be "shoved aside and forgotten because the report also said busing was the best tool to end racial segregation in schools, and that the state should extend no additional aid to non-public schools, particularly schools operated by the Roman Catholic Church."

Allen quoted one legislator as saying: "They're nuts. Don't they know this is an election year." [25]

It was even reported widely in the press that Rockefeller privately disavowed the commission report, saying that he had no idea the commission was going to go radical on him.

Finally in January 1973, after the commission had been duly thanked and relieved of further responsibility, the *New York Times* published a 1680-word OpEd story, authored by Manly Fleischmann and titled: "The Education of Manly Fleischmann." In it, Fleischmann presented an eloquent but low-key justification of the commission's conclusions. He framed this masterful article within the context of all the things he had been taught during three years of study. He acknowledged that the state was "almost $2-million poorer, the amount invested in the work," but he added the commission hoped it would "affect education in New York State importantly."

Some highlights of his powerful and moving defense of the commission, even as it was being discredited on all sides, follow:

"To our surprise, we discovered – and the discovery was repeated time and again in the course of our study – that there was no agreed upon body of goals, principles or practice in our system of public education. ... It did come as a shock to many of us to learn, for example, that after thousands of years of effort, there was still wide disagreement on such an elementary matter as the best method of teaching children to read. ...

"I was alarmed however to discover that New York State – as well as many other states – is encountering an unacceptably high rate of student failure, particularly in the acquisition of the three skills most essential to an effective adult life – reading, writing and arithmetic. ...

"I suppose my most shocking discovery in this area was the unfairness of the manner in which educational revenues are raised, and the greater inequity of the system under which these revenues are allocated. In my innocence, I had supposed that revenues were necessarily raised largely on the basis of ability to pay, and that distribution was on the basis of educational need. It never occurred to me that it would be possible in an enlightened state for affluent families to pay less in taxes for the education of their children than their lower-income neighbors in a nearby district. ...

"I had considered myself a reasonably informed citizen, but I simply could not have been made to believe that more than half of our identifiably handicapped children in New York State receive no special education of any kind. Neither did it seem possible that tens of thousands of non-English speaking children would be expected to learn in classrooms presided over by a teacher who spoke only English – but these are the sorry facts. ...

"Accountability, like motherhood, is a term that enjoys universal approval; the difficulty is that no one can agree as to just what accountability means in an educational system. ...

"Integration – A Lost Hope? In this area, I was subjected to a wholly different and painful kind of learning process during my years on the commission. Like so many other Americans, I completely misjudged the temper of the American people and the calculated purpose of the Nixon Administration to halt and then to reverse the steady progress of racial integration in the public schools in the South while simultaneously undermining efforts to check the trend toward increased segregation in the North. It soon became evident that Northern de facto segregationists were at least as heartless and determined as their Southern de jure counterparts. ..." [26]

After three years of passionate and painstaking work, rewarded with a barrage of criticism, much of it disingenuous, Manly Fleischmann did not mince his words.

"Manly was not bitter," recalled his colleague Odza. "But he did have negative feelings about it. Manly was a typical litigator. A typical litigator becomes so wrapped up in his client's cause and case that he becomes the cause and case and he believes in it fervently. He wraps himself up in it and it becomes almost emotional. Manly was that way. Manly became very wrapped up in this and he believed in it with his whole being. He took ownership. His greatest frustration was that the Legislature and the governor didn't recognize the importance of it; that this was the way out of their problem." [27]

In Fleischmann's obituary in the *New York Times*, John T. McQuiston summed it up saying the Fleischmann Commission report "aroused considerable controversy across the country. The report added to a nationwide debate on education, but few of its recommendations were adopted." [28]

Nevertheless, a federal judge in Buffalo would rule a few years later that the Buffalo Schools must be integrated through busing, and that the busing plan must pass the muster of the federal courts. And the State Legislature a decade later would make it the law that handicapped children be accommodated through special education, regardless of the nature of their handicap, and that foreign language students be taught reading, writing and arithmetic in their native language while they learned English. Several other states, like Michigan, have taken over the total cost of public education, while the allocation of school aid money continues to this day to be a bone in the throats of New York State legislators every year.

Fleischmann's colleague and partner William Schapiro might have said it best when he observed: "Manly knew there was going to be great opposition to this. … It was not a surprise. But Manly did what he knew was right: The right policy – not politically correct – the right policy." [29]

CHAPTER VI

The Group of 13:
The Founding Partners

The first day of January 1955 came and went and the Jaeckle firm remained in its offices in the Rand Building, downtown Buffalo's only legitimate sky-scraper.

At this time, the Jaeckle firm was officially Garono, Jaeckle, Kelly & Wick, but Ed Jaeckle of national political fame was its star. It was appropriate that the Jaeckle firm should be housed in the region's symbol of business power, the Rand Building, opened in 1929 with its dirigible landing tower that had been converted into the beacon for radio and television signals across Western New York.

Just down Main Street, in the block originally chosen by Holland Land Co. agent Joseph Ellicott as the center of the village of New Amsterdam, the Fleischmann brothers and their associates still occupied offices in the more aus-tere Ellicott Square Building. When opened in 1896, this 10-story structure, the work of architect Charles Atwood of the Chicago-based D. H. Burnham and Co., was described as the largest, finest and most complete office building in America. The bustling Ellicott Square, occupying the downtown block bounded by Main, Washington, Swan and Eagle streets, also was a prestigious location, suited for the firm that by now was officially Fleischmann, Augspurger, Campbell & Mugel.

The two firms had agreed in the fall of 1954 to merge and move into a new suite of offices on the 15th floor of the Rand Building, but the suite wasn't ready so the new year passed with the firms working cooperatively, but still in their old offices. J. B. Walsh recalls that it was April of 1955 before the two firms moved into their new offices – Jaeckle, Fleischmann, Kelly, Swart & Augspurger. Walsh specifically recalls that there were 13 lawyers in the new firm because, he joked, he ranked No. 13 in age and experience, the very bottom in the pecking order.[1]

If there were any special ceremonies on April 1, no one recorded the events and later, no one recalled ever hearing about them. John Wick, a Jaeckle partner, remembers moving from one office in the Rand Building to another, but he's not even sure there was a specific date set for the move. Adelbert Fleischmann and J.B. Walsh, a Fleischmann partner, remember moving up Main Street to the Rand Building, but neither could even recall their first meeting with Ed Jaeckle. In fact, it is not clear who initiated the merger. Ed Jaeckle and Manly Fleischmann had gained national reputations by this time, and both had extensive dealings with John Lord O'Brian. But it is not clear who drove the merger. What is clear is that the merger was not brokered by Adelbert Fleischmann. A half century later, Adelbert said he knew of Ed Jaeckle but didn't know him personally. Then flashing that hint of a smile, he revealed: "I was opposed to the merger. As you can see, I lost. But that's all right. Jaeckle had a good firm and it turned out, didn't it?" [2] When pressed for the motivation behind his opposition, he waved the back of a hand, indicating that it was too long ago to have any significance. He added: "There never were any arguments in the firm. Jaeckle ran it. He was the boss not only of the Republican Party but of Jaeckle Fleischmann."

Even though the actual merger apparently passed without ceremony, it is clear that by the Spring of 1955, some of Downtown Buffalo's most prestigious lawyers had come together in a new firm that would have an impact on the city, lasting into the 21st Century.

Owen B. Augspurger Jr.

This was not a merger of just Ed Jaeckle and Manly and Adelbert Fleischmann. Both of these firms had strong personnel, who had developed reputations in their own right. When Adelbert spoke of the members of this new firm, he said: "And first, of course, there was Owen Augspurger."

Owen B. Augspurger Jr. and Adelbert Fleischmann had been friends at Nichols and had spent their four years of World War II service together in the Pacific with the 102nd Anti-Aircraft Battalion in the Dutch East Indies, New Guinea and the Philippines. Augspurger had enlisted as a private and left active duty as a lieutenant colonel. He was outgoing, well-spoken and had all the characteristics of a natural leader. He was elected Delaware District councilman in 1949 at the age of 36. Adelbert recalled he was a good public speaker, "very gregarious" and "as bright as can be." In fact the two friends had half-fantasized about how Owen, the front man, would be elected mayor, governor and eventually president of the United States with Adelbert Fleischmann running his campaigns. "I would be attorney general," Adelbert said, adding a little sadly, "It never quite worked out." [3]

Augspurger was a graduate of Princeton University and the University of Buffalo Law School, class of 1937. He was the son of a prominent Buffalo businessman, Owen B. Augspurger, who was president of Merchants Mutual Casualty Co. when he was found dead of an apparent suicide in 1934. Before the war, young Owen was an associate with the law firm Falk, Phillips, Twelvetrees & Falk. During the war, he met and married Paula Norris of Brisbane, who was described in Buffalo newspapers as "a beautiful Australian girl."

"I met Paula in Brisbane in 1943, just before she joined the Australian Women's Army Service," Augspurger told a *Buffalo Evening News* reporter. "She was a staff sergeant and was chief of a cipher section ... When she was discharged recently, she held the rank of warrant officer." [4] He revealed to the newspaper in a 1945 interview that it had cost him $16 that day to talk to his wife in Australia "by long-distance" and that it would be several months before she could gain passage to the United States.

Augspurger had boundless energy and was a leader in everything he touched. He stayed active in the military after the war and by 1964, he was brigadier general in charge of the 5th Area Command in the New York Guard. He was active in Red Cross fund campaigns after the war and within a few years, he was serving on national Red Cross advisory panels and was vice chairman of the Red Cross National Convention in Seattle. He was chairman of the Buffalo Red Cross Chapter and served as the first chairman of the Buffalo Regional Blood Program. His Red Cross leadership role, along with his active participation in the Community Chest, Boy Scouts, the American Cancer Society, and the International Institute made him a natural driving force in 1960 for the merger of the major charitable and service organizations into the United Way of Buffalo and Erie County. He served as a United Way trustee until his death.

He was a director of Jones-Rich Milk, Roblin-Seaway Industries and the Buffalo Civic Auto Ramps, but his crowning achievement came through the Greater Buffalo Development Foundation and the Backers Realty. In the

1960s, Augspurger teamed up with Lee Norton, senior vice president of the Erie County Savings Bank, and R. J. (Chris) Schutz, president of Kleinhans, to put together the complex land package that resulted in the $20 million Main Place Mall and Erie County Savings Bank tower on Main Street between the Liberty Bank Building and Shelton Square. In naming Augspurger a Citizen of the Year for a second time in 1964, *The Buffalo Evening News* said the three men had "devoted their time without limit to the task and without the customary rewards of public service. ... Their efforts spearheaded the program that has now begun and will become a capstone in other downtown rejuvenation." [5]

Little known however was the fact that when the trio found a developer for the multi-million dollar project, the developer wanted to hire Augspurger as on-site counsel. His law colleague, William Schapiro, said Augspurger refused. "He had a very strong ethical sense about that. He said: 'I don't want people to think that my interest in this project has been to land the biggest client,'" Schapiro recalled. "That was a great client he gave up. It was not a little thing. ... But if he was to maintain that he was interested in Downtown Buffalo, and not in it to line his own pocket, he couldn't be promoting Main Place develop-ment and then wind up representing the developer. He wanted the right to ask people to do things for the public good. You destroy that if you wind up with the juiciest client." [6]

Augspurger took a special interest in the region's history, especially military history. He could be seen in full military regalia at Historical Society functions. He was elected president of the Buffalo & Erie County Historical Society in 1964, and was active in the effort to preserve the Wilcox Mansion on Delaware Avenue, where Theodore Roosevelt was sworn in as president upon the death of President McKinley. He would not live to see that home made a national historic site. *The Buffalo Evening News* said he combined his military and his-torical connections to "contribute enormously to U.S.-Canadian relations" and worked tirelessly on the 100th anniversary peace celebration between the two nations. [7]

In August of 1969, Western New York was shocked to learn that the young and vibrant Owen Augspurger, vacationing in Bozeman, Mont., with his family, had been thrown from a horse, and within days died of complications from a neck injury. Augspurger was known as a strong horseman. He had a farm with horses in Strykersville and members of the firm would bring their families there for weekend outings. He was only 56 years old on Aug. 9, 1969, when word came from a Bozeman hospital that Augspurger was dead.

"Owen played a big part in this firm," recalled Adelbert Fleischmann, with obvious sadness in his eyes more than 35 years later. "He was part of the firm's early Policy Committee. ..." His voice dropped off. [8]

Augspurger received awards too numerous to list during his lifetime, including the Samuel P. Capen award for outstanding service to the University of Buffalo Alumni, and after his death, he was named recipient of the Historical Society's Red Jacket Award and the society named a new community service award after him.

And when a new civic parking ramp was built in Downtown Buffalo, his colleague Paul C. Weaver recalled he had the idea that the ramp should be named for Augspurger, who had come up with the concept of civic auto ramps for Downtown Buffalo. "I had dealt with the Common Council on many occasions, but when I went in to propose that the new ramp be named for Owen, this was the only time I made my proposal, and bang, within ten seconds, it was accepted unanimously, no arguments, no questions, done." Then, by an accident of timing, according to Weaver, in the presence of Augspurger's wife and three children, Mayor Jimmy Griffin dedicated the new Owen B. Augspurger Jr. Ramp on Aug. 9, 1983, the 14th anniversary of his untimely death. [9]

Dwight Campbell

Another name that goes back to those turbulent post-war years is Dwight Campbell, a name that shows up on the Fleischmann-Augspurger letterhead soon after the Fleischmanns and Owen Augspurger set up shop in the Ellicott Square Building after the war. In fact, Campbell had been associated with Augspurger before the war when both were part of Falk, Phillips, Twelvetrees & Falk. But with America facing an active role in the war, Campbell enlisted in the Navy, while Augspurger went Army.

Campbell came to Buffalo from South Dakota where his father was a prominent railroad lawyer and later a member of the judiciary in South Dakota. Originally a generalist, Dwight, who also answered to "Dick" Campbell, migrated toward labor law and by the mid-'60s, he was considered the firm's leading labor lawyer.

It was Dwight Campbell who handled the integration of the Jaeckle and

Fleischmann firms in 1954-55, and Campbell became the combined firm's first managing partner, a task nobody wanted at that time. [10]   Ed Jaeckle was "very much in charge at the time," according to William Schapiro, "but he was not a micromanager. Ed was very content to let Dwight Campbell take care of the day-to-day things."   Campbell was still a managing partner in the Spring of 1969, when he announced he was leaving to start a new life as a yachtsman and charter boat operator in Florida. Both his parents had recently died and Dwight let it be known that he was calling it quits at age 52 and starting a new career on the seas.   He had a yacht constructed at a Long Island marina the previous summer and he and his son had sailed up the New England coast. The following Spring, he sailed it to Florida.

On May 4, 1999, when Dwight Campbell died, fellow founding partner Albert Mugel paid tribute to him in an office memo, citing his work on the merger and his years as a managing partner, adding: "Dick was not only one of the finest lawyers we have known, but was a lawyer and man of great principle."   It was noted that among his accomplishments, Campbell had organized and arranged the funding for the Buffalo Medical Foundation, the predecessor to the Hauptman-Woodward Foundation. [11]

On the Jaeckle Side: Kelly and Swart

The name Harry J. Kelly is associated with Jaeckle as early as 1935 when his name shows up as a named partner in Garono, Kelly, Jaeckle & Wick. Harry Kelly gained a reputation as a trial lawyer, defending local companies, notably the IRC transit company, and its successor, the NFT, against all comers for 40 years. Kelly achieved national prominence when he defended the old Bell Aircraft Corp. in what was billed as the first trial arising from the collision of commercial aircraft in the United States. Later, he defended Bell Aircraft in a case resulting from the explosion of a Bell helicopter in the air. [12]

Kelly was a year older than Ed Jaeckle. He was born on the city's West Side on July 29, 1893, to a successful Irish immigrant, Patrick J. Kelly, and Nellie McMullen Kelly. The elder Kelly had teamed up with Mathias Hens in 1893 to start a dry goods business that became known as the Hens & Kelly department store. Young Harry Kelly grew up in Holy Angels parish and attended Nardin Academy, Lafayette High School and Georgetown University before earning a law degree from the University of Buffalo Law School in 1920. At

Georgetown, Kelly was an All-American pitcher and part of a famous collegiate battery of Kelly and Cuff.

Kelly served in the Navy in World War I as a lieutenant (jg) and after the war, he was associated with the law firm of Lock, Babcock, Spratt & Hollister, and later, Dudley Stowe & Sawyer before teaming up with Garono and Jaeckle. [13]

Elected a fellow in the American College of Trial Lawyers in 1956, Kelly was said to have participated in more than 2000 cases that went to trial. Even so, he insisted it usually was better to settle a case out of court whenever possible. In 1962, Kelly recalled a case where he had been ready to settle for $25,000 when a jury came back, asking the court for further instructions. The jury foreman asked if they were allowed to award the plaintiff more than he sought. When the judge instructed that the amount named in the suit was the maximum they could award, any chance for a settlement went out the courtroom door. Then 10 minutes later, to Kelly's surprise, the jury came back and awarded the plaintiff $10,000. When Kelly sought out some of the jurors later to inquire about their question, it is said they told him: "We were just curious … so we decided to ask the judge." Kelly concluded: "You never know what a jury will do." [14]

Kelly was a director of the Sterling Amherst Farms Dairy, a early home deliverer of dairy products, whose uniformed milkmen could be seen any morning in North Buffalo and the northern suburbs in the late 1940s. He also was president of the Buffalo Athletic Club, and served as treasurer until his death of the Ellicott Club, the holding company for the BAC.

Harry Kelly and the former Helen Madigan had eight children and Kelly was proud to tell any listener about his trip to Louvain, Belgium, for the ordination of his son James G. Kelly to the priesthood. Monsignor Kelly, recalling his childhood in Kenmore, noted that when he was baptized, his godfather was Buffalo Mayor Joseph Kelly, who was no relation, and his godmother was Grace Jaeckle, the boss's wife. [15]

Colleague Paul Weaver remembered walking with Kelly from the Liberty Bank Building offices to the courthouse on several occasions. Kelly would stride down the street, wearing his patented straw hat, and reading the file on the case he was about to argue as he walked. "He was a marvelous trial lawyer," said Weaver. "There he is reading the file as he walked and he'd have the whole file memorized by the time he got into the courtroom. He was considered the dean of the trial bar back in the late fifties and sixties." [16]

In typical Kelly fashion, when he was hospitalized in 1964, he had his secretary come to his hospital bed to finish up some outstanding briefs. Upon his death on June 21, 1964, Justice Hamilton Ward, administrative judge of the Eighth Judicial District, described Harry Kelly as "one of the giants of the trial bar." Justice Ward urged the younger trial lawyers to pattern themselves after Kelly, saying Kelly was "a gentleman at all times. He had a proper courtesy toward his opponents, proper courtesy and deference toward the Court. By that I don't mean a bowing or conceding attitude toward the Court, but a proper attitude." [17]

Joseph Swart

Another of the Jaeckle partners who came into the new merged firm in 1955 was Joseph Swart, a corporate lawyer who represented a long list of Buffalo companies. Swart, the son of a Medina farmer, was born in 1901 and came to Buffalo to attend high school at St. Joseph's Collegiate Institute, the Christian Brothers high school on Main Street at the time. He graduated from the UB Law School and was admitted to the bar in 1921.

Swart began his career with the blue-blood Shire & Jellinek firm in the Prudential Building. Then, after a period of practicing with former state Supreme Court Justice David Diamond, he joined up with Ed Jaeckle in 1953 and that firm changed its name to Garono, Jaeckle, Kelly & Swart. The Swart name, like the Kelly name, remained as part of the Jaeckle Fleischmann merger until about 1970, although Swart died at age 65 on Feb. 5, 1966.

Swart had been a managing partner for a time and was a director of the Loblaws grocery chain. He also was on the boards of Jafco Marina, Sol Lenzner Corp., Sage Equipment, and Meyer Malt, the producer of malt for Buffalo's many breweries. And he was a trustee of the Frauenheim Foundation.

A Navy veteran and a captain in the National Guard, Swart served as a hearing officer on appeals by conscientious objectors from 1958 to 1963.

Joe Swart was known as a problem solver. "In a couple of exotic cases, he was the one who was able to figure out what the law was and how it applied," recalled Paul Weaver. And Swart's son, Michael, who was with the Jaeckle Fleischmann firm from 1969 to 1980 ultimately becoming a partner, remembered Manly Fleischmann telling young Swart how his father had been the one who figured out what to do when an American Airlines plane was seized by the U.S. government at Buffalo Airport as evidence in a crime. Adelbert Fleischmann described Swart as "one of the best general practitioners. He could do just about anything." [18]

Albert R. Mugel: One of a Kind

Professor Albert Mugel had a hypnotizing effect on his students. He was a storyteller, serious and straight-forward one minute and seemingly lost in complex legal thought the next. But it was that cigarette, burning inextricably toward his lips while he talked, that mesmerized some students. Knowing he wouldn't touch it until the smoldering ash reached his lips, they would place penny bets on the number of seconds it might take for the ash to fall from that ever-present cigarette, and more often than not when it did fall, it would leave a small brown mark on his tie or shirt. A colleague remarked that every shirt and tie the man owned had little brown holes burned in them from cigarette ashes. His courses on tax law, future interests and estate planning covered some pretty dry material but for two generations of law students at the University of Buffalo, his storytelling ability and his dry wit won over the day. Mugel's classes usually were limited to 8 o'clock Friday and Saturday mornings so he could spend the rest of the week at his law practice. It wasn't unusual for the two-hour Saturday class to break up at about noon, and the Friday class ended when the students, queued up outside the door for the next class, caused so much commotion that they finally distracted the professor. Without a doubt, Al Mugel was one of a kind. [19]

Mugel was born Oct. 10, 1917, to a West Side Buffalo couple. He lived on Prospect Avenue and later at 23 Park St. His son, Richard, recalled his father saying that he used to roller skate on the slate sidewalks on Delaware Avenue. Mugel attended Holy Angels School, St. Joseph's Collegiate Institute and Canisius College before receiving his law degree from UB in 1941. He practiced law briefly before entering the Army in World War II, serving as a tank officer with the 717th Tank Battalion and seeing action in France and Belgium. He liked to tell his friends that he fell into the Rhine while the rest of his battalion was crossing it, but the truth is, the Germans blew up the Rhine bridge as the last of the battalion supplies were being moved across from France. [20] He would be recalled into the Army for a short time during the Korean conflict.

After the war, Mugel began teaching at UB and befriended a slightly older part-time lecturer at the school, Manly Fleischmann. In 1954, Manly and his brother Adelbert enticed Mugel to join their downtown law firm, Fleischmann, Augspurger & Campbell, and he did with the proviso that he could continue teaching at UB. So for a year before the Jaeckle - Fleischmann merger, the Fleischmann firm became Fleischmann, Augspurger, Campbell & Mugel. Mugel would be an icon in the merged firm for almost 50 years, but his name would not emerge as part of the firm name again until about 1970, after the deaths of Kelly, Swart and Augspurger.

Mugel had a keen legal mind. In fact, his colleagues all used the same word to describe him: Brilliant. He was a director of Trico Products and was instrumental in setting up the legal architecture for the family's John R. Oishei Foundation. Mugel had a particular interest in the foundation as a catalyst for change in the city right up to his death. He also was a director of Confer Plastics, the Library Foundation, the Buffalo Club, the High Street Center, the Buffalo General Foundation and Aeroil Products. He was a tireless worker, but as colleague Paul Weaver put it: "If Al practiced law on his own, he'd have starved to death. He never sent out a bill. Adelbert [Fleischmann] was the guy who would go to him at the end of every year and plead with him to get the bills out." Another colleague, Michele Heffernan, recalled his great sense of fairness. "Even a bill became a huge project. It had to be fair and it had to be right." [21]

"Al was a unique personality," recalled Randy Odza. He was "a difficult personality in many respects, but a wonderful personality all at the same time. A very complex person, a typical Manly Fleischmann protégé, a brilliant man." [22]

Almost without trying, Mugel was the recruiter of much of the Jaeckle Fleischmann talent. Heffernan put it simply: "Al Mugel is the reason I'm here." Paul Weaver and William Schapiro repeated those sentiments. John Montfort was another Mugel recruit. Schapiro spoke of the late evening sessions with Mugel and "his acolytes," of which he was one. Others at various times included John Putnam, Timothy Leixner, Ronald H. Jensen, Paul A. Battaglia and Thomas Palmer. Schapiro said young lawyers would have dinner with Mugel and work into the night because it was an honor to be part of his group. Schapiro described him as "the last-word lawyer." When a person wanted to get the last word on a subject, they would go to someone like him. "That's what Al was – the last-word lawyer." [23]

At times, it was difficult to determine where the law ended and the Mugel social conscience kicked in. During his long sessions with his acolytes, he would diverge into philosophy and sociology. It was not unusual for Mugel to move from inheritance taxes and estate planning to the problems facing aging Buffalo business owners.

For example, Mugel thought that one of the problems Buffalo shared with similar cities was rooted in the obsession of family business owners with the notion that to die while still owning a successful business meant ruination because of unreasonable and punitive estate taxes. He laid much of the blame for this obsession at the feet of insurance companies which he thought painted a one-dimensional picture of what might happen if a businessman were to die before he sold his business. Their answer of course, he would say, is unreasonably expensive insurance policies. He thought the concept of selling out the good and profitable business a person created to a conglomerate out of fear of death taxes was an impediment to long-term business growth in Buffalo. He would argue long and vociferously to persuade his colleagues that there were a variety of alternatives from which to choose, and selling out for fear of death was not high on that list of alternatives. [24]

He would point to trusts, foundations and advance gifting as just a few of the estate planning tools available and he worked tirelessly to put his theories into practice.

For all his successes in estate planning, one big one apparently got away. It is significant that Ed Jaeckle was a close friend, counselor and confidante to the owner, the editor and two publishers of the region's chief media outlet, *The Buffalo Evening News*, as well as a director of the company. Al Mugel and John Putnam were considered the best one-two punch for estate planning in the region, and by the 1970s, Mugel's reputation in legal circles was national. Yet in the definitive history of the newspaper, *From Butler to Buffett*, by long-time *News* editor Murray B. Light, Light claims that despite constant pleas from friends and legal advisers, it was a poorly managed estate that ended the Butler family ownership of the newspaper, television and radio outlets. "For years, Kate [Mrs. Edward H.] Butler had repeatedly rejected the advice of her attorneys that she take steps to minimize the tax consequences that would occur upon her death," Light wrote. "All [of her advisers] told her that it was important that she gift some of her assets before death. If she failed to do this, she was advised a 'fire sale' of the paper would result to satisfy the estate taxes. She stubbornly refused." [25]

And a fire sale it was. When Mrs. Butler died in August 1974, the Butler heirs agreed to sell the newspaper for a reported $35.5 million to Warren E. Buffett, who later would become a legendary investor and the second richest man in the nation. Ed Jaeckle, Ron Jensen and Randy Odza would be among those representing the Butler interests and Mugel would be the lead lawyer in charge of the sale for the heirs. Twenty-five years later, the value of that newspaper property would be estimated by the paper's chief financial officer in the hundreds of millions of dollars. Incidentally, Odza remained involved as one of the newspaper's labor lawyers under the Buffett ownership, and he became a trusted counselor to News publisher Stanford Lipsey. And Jensen, after nearly 25 years with the firm, became a professor at the Pace University Law School in New York City, where he was teaching various courses on tax law in 2006.

A semi-pro baseball pitcher in his younger days, it was not unusual for Mugel to show up and pitch a few innings for the Jaeckle Fleischmann softball team. He would be in his street clothes, dress shoes and he'd have the ever-present cigarette in his mouth, even on the mound. A would-be protégé, Edward Piwowarczyk, who went into the labor practice, recalls the wry Mugel humor. "We were having a beer after a baseball game and I must have gotten a little too presumptuous. Al pointed to the words on my baseball shirt and without cracking a smile said: 'Just remember, the Mugel printed on that shirt is me.'" [26]

Al Mugel retired from the firm two years before his death when his always poor eyesight reached the point where he was legally blind, and his hearing began to fail. Even so, he continued teaching until his death on Sept. 10, 2003. In life, he had received UB's Samuel P. Capen Alumni Award and the Law School's highest honor, the Jaeckle Award, named after his colleague and friend, Ed Jaeckle. He also has a prestigious competition, the Mugel National Tax Moot Court Competition, named in his honor. Of his death, the dean of the UB Law School, Nils Olsen, said: "It's a great loss not only to the university and the Law School, but also to the legal profession." [27] Looking back, James Tanous, chairman of the firm's executive committee at the time of Mugel's death, said: "Al was always a deep breath. The firm owes a tremendous amount to him because he did spectacular things ... but you can only have one Al at a time. And you're fortunate if you have one Al. You're so much better off for having had him." [28]

The Remaining Five

The remainder of the original 13 partners in the merged firm were Louis DelCotto, John Wick, John Cox, Cyril Kavanaugh and J.B. Walsh.

Lou DelCotto became a tax authority in his own right, but he didn't remain long with Jaeckle Fleischmann. He came up through the Fleischmann branch of the firm, after graduating from the UB Law School in 1951. But before 1960, DelCotto was off to Columbia University on a Ford Fellowship, and after receiving a master's degree there, he began a 40-year teaching career at the UB Law School. He went on to receive the Law School's Jaeckle Award and upon his death in April 2005, the UB *Link* wrote that he was "instrumental in extensively shaping and defining the tax curriculum at the law school for more than 40 years." [29]

It is noteworthy that the name "Wick" in the 1952 Jaeckle firm name is not the same Wick who would partner in the merged Jaeckle Fleischmann firm. Charles J. Wick and his younger brother John Wick grew up on Blaine Avenue on the city's East Side. Both brothers were taught by the Jesuit fathers at Canisius High School and Canisius College before earning their law degrees at UB. Charles Wick was a named partner in the Ed Jaeckle firm in 1952, but in 1953, Charles became regional vice president of the Niagara Mohawk Power Co. He held that position in 1956 when the Schoellkopf Power Station broke off the side of the Niagara Gorge and slid onto the rocks below, an event that would lead to the massive Niagara Power Project further down river. Charles Wick spent the rest of his long career with the power company and remained friends with Ed Jaeckle, who was a director of the power company. [30]

John Wick was a partner in the Jaeckle firm in the Rand Building when the merger occurred in 1955. John remained with Jaeckle Fleischmann until 1963 when he left for a position at Merchants Mutual, where he eventually became company president. Jaeckle also was a director of that firm and John Wick became a director of the power company. The three remained friends until Jaeckle's death. In retirement, John Wick became a deacon in the Catholic Church.

John Cox was described as a flamboyant lawyer who came up on the Jaeckle branch of the merged firm. Cox broke off and formed his own firm about 1957 and practiced in the Buffalo area for many years before his death. Cy Kavanaugh was an older member of the Jaeckle firm and worked in estate planning with the new firm until his death. A colorful associate, Robert White, also came over from the Jaeckle firm. A close friend of Al Mugel, White left in the early 1960s. The merger even affected the office staff, with Catherine Barone, Jaeckle's office manager, and Ione Marseilles, the Fleischmann office manager, not always seeing eye to eye.

The youngest lawyer in the merged firm was J.B. Walsh, who had a storied career as lawyer, cruise ship entertainer, Justice Department lawyer in Washington, lobbyist for the City of Buffalo and judicial candidate. In 2006, he was in-house counsel for Ecology & Environment in Lancaster.

Walsh joined the Fleischmann firm in 1954 after receiving his law degree from the Georgetown University Law School. He recalls making the move to the Rand Building in the Spring of 1955. J.B. was an amateur songwriter and he played the piano and sang with a hefty voice. It was J.B. who wrote and sang, with the future Federal Judge John O. Henderson, lyrics to the tune of: "I Want a Girl, Just Like the girl …" But his lyrics, in honor of Ed Jaeckle's role in the sale of the Statler Hotel empire, were:

> "I want a fee,
> Just like the fee
> They got from Statler's Trust." [31]

John O. Henderson, while not a part of the merger, had been associated with the Fleischmanns in the early 1950s when the firm was Fleischmann, Augspurger, Henderson & Campbell, and then later, Cohen, Fleischmann, Augspurger, Henderson & Campbell. In 1953, Henderson was the surprise choice of President Eisenhower for U.S. attorney from the Western District of New York. By 1959, this son of English and Scots immigrants was a federal judge, a position he held until his death in 1974. His youthful exuberance and boisterous humor never left Judge Henderson and it was noted in 1974 that his abrupt quips, his stories and his zesty humor kept court staff and lawyers for all sides at the ready. [32]

The Cohen whose named showed up briefly on the Fleischmann letterhead was Paul Cohen, a partner in a leading Niagara Falls firm who split off and joined the Fleischmanns in the early '50s. That association didn't last very long and Cohen split off again to form a partnership with his nephew, Robert Swados.

Walsh stayed with Jaeckle Fleischmann until the Spring of 1960 when he went off to Washington for a brief fling with the Anti-Trust Division of the Justice Department. Walsh returned to the firm in 1975 when Jaeckle Fleischmann opened an Albany office to handle local lobbying needs. He split his time between Buffalo and Albany until that office was closed about 1980.

It was J.B. Walsh who put flesh and blood on an oft-told Jaeckle tale that was repeated by colleagues and friends over the years, sometimes citing different clients, different situations and different fees, but always with the same punch line. According to Walsh, a tough Buffalo businessman had been trying for months to gain approval of a minor technical change from a state agency that would result in a lucrative contract. This almost meaningless alteration represented the closing chapter in what had been a months-long saga of bureaucratic red tape, culminating in Albany's favorite game – pass the buck from office to office. Jaeckle listened to the particulars of his client's problem and then excused himself to make a phone call. Within minutes, Jaeckle was back in the room with the good news: It was done; the client got what he wanted. After smiles and expressions of amazement, the client, knowing there would be a bill to pay, is said to have asked: "How much will this cost me?" When Jaeckle told the client he'd receive a bill for $5,000, the client is said to have protested: "With all due respect, twenty minutes of your time, Mr. Jaeckle, and one phone call is worth five thousand bucks?" Jaeckle is said to have answered: "It's okay, pal. Forget it ever happened. I can make another phone call." [33]

Years later, Ed Piwowarczyk would recall Jaeckle ingraining in his young associates the attitude that it is not the time you spend on a client's case, "it's results that you charge for."

CHAPTER VII

The Sum of the Parts Times Ten

The question is inevitable. And the answer quickly becomes obvious. Who stood to gain from the merger of these two starkly different firms? Each was headed by a strong-minded national celebrity. Each had tasted success in its own right. So why merge?

Ed Jaeckle probably put it most concisely when he is said to have exclaimed: "It was a very logical merger. I had the clients and they had the brains." [1] And from the Fleischmann perspective, Judge John Henderson, who had already left the Fleischmanns for a career in public service by 1955, told a young colleague looking to join the firm that the Fleischmanns had been living hand to mouth while Jaeckle had plenty of money. For them, a piece of the Jaeckle bank account was something to be treasured. [2]

Adelbert Fleischmann, the master of understatement, would only chuckle when reminded of Henderson's characterizations. "I've heard that story," Adelbert said. Jaeckle "got a bunch of good lawyers when he joined up with my brother and me, and a few others." Adelbert added later, "We had some very good lawyers in our firm. Well I think we were the top business firm, but I'm prejudiced."

Long-time chairman William Schapiro said that Jaeckle just had a knack for attracting money. He never feared asking for compensation commensurate with his value to the client. Jaeckle could pick up the phone and the state attorney general would come out of a meeting to answer his call. In later years, Gov. Nelson Rockefeller was known to personally place after-hours calls to the Jaeckle Fleischmann receptionist, looking for Ed. [3] So Ed Jaeckle just naturally attracted a lot of up-and-coming Buffalo business people.

"The rainmaker; that was Jaeckle," is how James Tanous put it. "He didn't practice law. I heard him say it many times. I've got wonderful lawyers here. I've got Bill Schapiro. Or maybe you need John Montfort." The always straight-talking Ralph Halpern said of Jaeckle: "He wouldn't have known where the law library was. But he knew about getting clients." And when he turned on the charm, he could be as charming as anyone in the profession. Jaeckle would never deprecate another lawyer to a potential client. In fact, if he wanted you, he would praise your current counsel while pointing out that as you grew and as your business became more complex, you would need services beyond the scope of your current counsel, services that only Jaeckle Fleischmann could supply. [4] "He was the best business-getter I've ever seen, any time, anywhere," recalled Halpern.

But as natural as it came to him, it was not without a conscious strategy. Jaeckle had grown up in Buffalo's upwardly-mobile German community. His young business friends were naturals for the German-American Bank of Buffalo. Yet, he recognized the need to appeal to a wider clientele. In the early 1970s, he remarked to a young Ed Piwowarczyk, who later became managing partner and executive committee chairman: "That's Polish isn't it? Well that's good. I believe in diversity." He didn't want to be labeled the German firm or the Jewish firm or the Italian firm or the Polish firm. "I think he was sincere," said Piwowarczyk. "He thought the collegiality of a mixture of people of different backgrounds strengthened the firm ... of course he was always marketing."

Manly Fleischmann was no slouch at drumming up business either. His national reputation attracted big business and he used his common partnership in the Buffalo firm and a New York City firm to leverage work back home. But Manly had an entirely different personality from Ed Jaeckle – many would say perfectly complementary. Manly had a very strong personality but he never was long on chit-chat. Odza described him as the stereotypical litigator, very tough but with a disarming sense of humor. Halpern, who was a partner in the firm headed by rival Frank G. Raichle at the time, would meet Manly on an American Airlines flight to LaGuardia. "He did a lot of socializing with clients in New York and he would say he spent too much time on the cocktail circuit chasing clients. I could only gather that was not what he wanted to do."

And then there was Adelbert Fleischmann who was universally described as the great humanizing force in the firm. Ed Jaeckle and brother Manly were in Adelbert's office on a regular basis, usually discussing personnel. Yet the newest associate in the firm felt comfortable knocking on Adelbert's door. It is said that Jaeckle told a colleague: "People underestimate Adelbert. He's a smart guy and because his brother is so famous, people make the wrong assumption about Delbert." [5]

The Liberty Bank: Following the Client

Within two years of setting up shop in new Rand Building offices, the firm saw a need to move, not because they outgrew their quarters but because of a new client which would remain key to Jaeckle Fleischmann for decades. The old German-American Bank of Buffalo had been chartered in 1882 and capitalized primarily by investment from the Fruit Belt community that was growing in numbers and becoming increasingly prosperous. After World War I, the bank facing Main Street at the corner of Court Street reacted to the anti-German sentiment sweeping the nation by changing its name to the Liberty Bank of Buffalo. Then in 1925, it built a landmark building on an expanded Main-Court site, overlooking the city's business and government centers. To dispel all doubt in the minds of investors about its patriotism, the building's twin towers, easily visible from Lemon Street, were topped by replicas of the Statue of Liberty. The bank, which would later become Liberty National, then Norstar Bank, then Fleet Bank and then be merged with the Bank of America, had a long association with the local law firm Wilcox & Van Allen. But by the end of the decade of the '50s, both named partners had died and E. Perry Spink, the new president of Liberty, sought the services of Ed Jaeckle and Manly Fleischmann's firm.

In late 1957, Jaeckle Fleischmann absorbed what remained of Wilcox & Van Allen – notably Sonny Gardner, Clint Sweet and Arch Laidlaw – and within a year moved to offices on the 7th floor of the Liberty Bank Building. Paul Weaver, who started with the firm in 1963 at a $6300 annual salary, recalled hearing there were 16 partners when that last merger was completed. The firm would spend most of the next two decades at Liberty Bank, expanding to the 8th floor, and changing its name after the deaths of Kelly, Swart and Augspurger to Jaeckle, Fleischmann & Mugel. It is generally believed that the name change was contemplated in 1972 when Manly was completing his work on the state's Fleischmann Commission report, but the official change may not have been finalized until 1973. By 1974 when Michele Heffernan joined the firm out of UB Law School, there were 36 lawyers in the two-level Jaeckle, Fleischmann & Mugel suites overlooking Main Street on one side, and Niagara

Square and City Hall on the other side.

One of those absorbed into the firm, Sonny Gardner, had gained a reputation through the bank as a real estate specialist. His true first name was Sunderland and he lived with his wife, Mary, on Lafayette Avenue. Heffernan described him as tall, calm and by the 1970s, a man with a full head of white hair. "He was so calm and so organized," Heffernan recalls. "People would be calling him saying this or that needed to happen by tomorrow, and his answer would be: 'I'm sorry but it isn't going to happen.'" Adelbert Fleischmann said his reputation as a real estate lawyer was so widely known that when he died, the clerks at County Hall presented his widow with a commemorative metal gadget used for voiding the old real estate tax stamps after closing. Heffernan, who became the firm's first female partner, inherited Gardner's office when he retired, the office "with a perfect view in every direction." Heffernan joined the firm the same day President Gerald Ford signed the ERISA legislation and became known for her expertise in employee benefits. She said she won the prize office the same way she gained the distinction of the being the first female partner: "Just by being there." She added: "It could just as well have been Gayle [Eagen] or Jean [Powers]."

Clint Sweet, whose real name was George C. Sweet, did corporate and estate work for Liberty and later for Jaeckle Fleischmann. He was about the same age as Jaeckle and had served in France during World War I. He told colleagues that he was with the bank during the October '29 crash, and that later, when President Roosevelt declared a bank holiday, Sweet remained at the bank several days and nights getting all the records organized for the bank reopening. Paul Weaver, who was president of Wanakah Country Club in the '70s, said he ran across some club records signed by its first treasurer, a George C. Sweet. When he inquired, Clint confirmed that the club's first treasurer was in fact his father. Clint recalled when he was five or six years old, standing on the hill at Wanakah with his dad, and looking across the bay toward Buffalo, where they saw an amazing sight that was burned into his childhood memory: The reflection of electric lights against the night clouds, giving off an entirely different glow than that of the usual gas lamps, the reflection from the Pan American Exposition in Delaware Park. And then what must have seemed a day or two later in a child's memory, he recalled workers placing sound-deadening material on Delaware Avenue to muffle the noise of carriage traffic outside the home of

John Milburn, where President William McKinley lay dying from an assassin's bullet. [6]

Later in the 1980s, when the firm moved out of the Liberty Bank Building, it was following the bank to new quarters in what became known as 12 Fountain Plaza at the end of the 20th Century. That move was accomplished in 1983 and 1984 with Daniel E. Wendt serving as firm administrator, and managing partner Timothy Leixner shepherding the involved process which dragged the firm – some say kicking and screaming – fully into the computer age. Heffernan recalls Leixner, who seemed to have a hard hat on his head or in his hand for two years, showing fellow lawyers around the skeleton of a new building and explaining the maze of wires that would move information around the 7th and 8th floors of the new office. Ed Piwowarczyk described Leixner as "probably ahead of his time," both technically and as a marketer. Technically, Leixner worked with the New York State Bar Association in the early development of the LexisNexis database which became the standard for law office use. A corporate lawyer, he handled the giant Peter J. Schmidt grocer account, but probably will be best remembered for negotiating the rights to build a covered walkway over West Huron Street connecting 12 Fountain Plaza and the Hyatt Regency Hotel. Leixner left the firm in 1987 and ultimately became a partner in the firm Holland & Knight in Florida. [7]

The New York City Connection

Manly Fleischmann kept an apartment in New York City, starting before the 1955 merger, and the firm maintained the apartment into the late 1980s. Just about everyone in the firm in the '50s, '60s and '70s has a story to tell about the New York apartment. But they aren't all talking about the same apartment. Alison Fleischmann talks about the place on 52nd Street. When Ralph Halpern spent the night before his wedding in the apartment, it was on East 57th Street. When Jim Tanous spent part of his honeymoon at the apartment, it was on Second Avenue. That's the apartment at East 47th Street and Second Avenue, where Randy Odza recalls waking up to the sight of Manly Fleischmann in his undershirt, holding a cereal bowl in one hand and fly swatter in the other hand, chasing a roach.

"Daddy loved New York City," said daughter Alison. "But originally, he was there in a desperate attempt to make a living." She explained that after Manly

Fleischmann left the War Production Board in 1952, the family moved to New York and Manly formed the partnership of Fleischmann, Stokes & Hitchcock. He started to commute between Buffalo and New York the following year, and after the reorganization of the New York firm in 1961, he was a common partner in the Buffalo firm and in Webster, Sheffield, Fleischmann, Hitchcock & Chrystie, with offices at One Rockefeller Plaza. Webster Sheffield was known as a very white shoe law firm that traced its roots back to the Civil War. The dual arrangement continued to Fleischmann's death when the name of the firm had been shortened to Webster & Sheffield. According to Alison Fleischmann, her father had addresses on Fifth Avenue, on East 52nd Street, at 340 East 57th Street and finally a block from the United Nations Building at East 47th Street and Second Avenue. [8]

So for 30 years, Manly Fleischmann split his time between Buffalo and New York City. He usually left Buffalo for LaGuardia on Monday evening and returned to Buffalo Thursday night, spending Friday to mid-day Monday at the Buffalo office. The trip was made easier by the fact that in May of 1956, he was named a director of American Airlines and thereafter usually was seated in Row 1, where he was known to conduct business with fellow commuters. He also was a director of the Equitable Life Assurance Society and the Sidney Blumenthal Company, headquartered in New York. [9]

The ever-frugal Adelbert Fleischmann saw the New York apartment as an opportunity. Adelbert would parlay the apartment ("being my brother, we had preference"), plus the American Airlines directorship ("I could buy coach tickets and get them upgraded to first class"), and his dealings with Maury Yellen, brother of Buffalo songwriter Jack Yellen ("We saw shows you couldn't buy tickets to") into inexpensive holidays. "I didn't know Jack Yellen very well," Adelbert confided. It is appropriate that Jack is probably best known for his song "Happy Days are Here Again."

Manly's common partner arrangement meant big business for the firm back in Buffalo. Bill Schapiro explained that Webster & Sheffield represented many socially prominent people. The Ford and the Rockefeller foundations were on their client list and John Lindsay was a partner before and after his two terms as mayor of New York. They didn't dirty their hands with labor law, some of which flowed to Buffalo, and Al Mugel did some high level tax work for corporations handled by Webster & Sheffield. It eventually became common for

Jaeckle Fleischmann partners in Buffalo to be working with Webster & Sheffield clients around the country.

Randy Odza, who had worked for a brief time at Proskauer, Rose in New York City, between the time he graduated from Cornell University and his arrival in Buffalo in 1969, recognized the opportunity that Webster & Sheffield represented for the Buffalo firm. "I kept pushing Manly, until eventually he introduced me to the partners down there and I started doing their labor work for them," explained Odza. That is how Carnegie Hall came to be represented by Odza, and Liggett & Myers Tobacco Co., by members of the Jaeckle Fleischmann firm. "And that's how I started to work for Mazda U.S.," recalled Odza.

Colleague Schapiro said: "Everyone talks about the Toyota-GM labor agreement in California [as changing the American auto industry], but the better agreement was the one hammered out at Mazda in Michigan by Odza and the UAW. That truly was a landmark agreement." Odza explained that Mazda made it known that it wanted to build a plant in the United States, but Mazda executives felt the company wasn't financially strong enough to operate under U.S. work rules or to buck the United Auto Workers. So Mazda executives and Tom Field of Webster & Sheffield went to UAW president Owen Bieber and told him Mazda was considering coming to the U.S., but only if an acceptable labor agreement could be bargained. The lion's share of the company bargaining fell to Odza. At first, the UAW offered the Toyota-GM model but a quietly stubborn Odza determined that that agreement was not specific enough to allow Mazda to undertake the burden of a U.S. plant. In the end, Odza and Steven Yokich, who later would become UAW president, negotiated a deal where instead of 110 union job classifications in a plant, there would be just two. Odza insists that this contract was not the "breakthrough agreement." That had been reached in California. "But we put teeth in that agreement, a more significant break," he said. And it then became the model for GM, Ford and Chrysler who insisted, if the UAW could do it for Mazda, they needed it too. [10]

After more than 20 years of commuting between New York and Buffalo, Manly Fleischmann would tell his Harvard classmates in the 50th anniversary report of his graduating class: "I currently find myself literally busier than ever and with no intentions of changing my life until compelled to do so by a higher authority." Of his "frenzied existence," he said: "I can truthfully reply that the only reason is that I enjoy it." Then in true Manly

Fleischmann style, this man who cherished the infrequent quiet of salmon fishing, added: "My only major disappointment in life has been my inability to acquire a salmon stream." [11]

Satellite Offices: Staying Close to the Business

When confronted with the question of the need for satellite offices, Adelbert Fleischmann was quick to make his point. He flashed his trademark mischievous smile and said his brother had established a satellite office in New York City before the Jaeckle Fleischmann merger occurred. The people at Webster & Sheffield might question his definition of satellite office, but the point was well taken.

Jaeckle Fleischmann has established offices over the years when there was a perceived need and closed them when the need no longer existed. In the 1970s, there was the Albany office, manned by J.B. Walsh and for a time, a second person. That office was closed when the anticipated lobbying business didn't meet expectations. In 1985, a Washington Office, specializing in antitrust and environmental work, was opened in an attractive location at 2000 Pennsylvania Ave. William P. Tedards Jr. and William L. Kovacs were resident partners, assisted by associate Mario Herman. James Tanous recalls being at that office the day President Ronald Reagan ordered the bombing of Libya, April 15, 1986. At the time, security barriers, the kind the nation has grown to accept after 9/11, hadn't been erected around Washington, and Tanous wondered why all the garbage trucks were moving down Pennsylvania Avenue toward the White House. The next day, newspapers around the country published photos of the makeshift garbage truck barrier set up around the White House. For a time, the Washington Office represented Media General, but it was closed after about four years when it failed to meet expectations.

There also was a one-person Batavia Office in the 1980s at 10 Ellicott St., headed by resident partner Stephen B. Hughes, but that lasted only as long as the special need it was set up to service.

The Amherst Office was opened in the late 1990s, partly to service a long-standing client, the Ciminelli Development Co. of Amherst, and to act as a traditional satellite office with close ties to Fountain Plaza headquarters. The office at 400 Essjay Road specializes in corporate law, real estate, corporate tax planning, and contract and construction litigation.

The firm also is experimenting with a Phoenix Office, headed by Ronald Kisicki, a former General Motors engineer who specializes in patents and emerging businesses.

The Rochester satellite office, founded in 1991 in the Ellwanger & Barry Building in downtown Rochester, began as a small all-purpose satellite office, but over the next 15 years, the office morphed into something quite different. In 2006, then-chairman James Tanous described the satellite, which by then had relocated to 190 Linden Oaks in the suburban Town of Penfield, as "a most exciting growth opportunity for the firm."

The office, under Rochester managing partner J. Montieth Estes, a former high-tech business owner known as "Monty," became the firm's center for patent work and developed a niche practice, specializing in creating, nurturing and growing emerging technology companies along the I-90 corridor from Buffalo to Albany.

For Jaeckle Fleischmann, there is no mystery to the establishment of satellite offices. When they are good for the business – when they serve to maintain strong contacts with a long-term client or when they can show a potential for growing the business – then satellite offices are good. If they serve no useful purpose, then they are redundant. The philosophy has not changed since Manly Fleischmann chose to spend half the week in Buffalo and half the week in New York City.

Ed and Manly: They didn't do it alone

If the Ed Jaeckle strategy of attracting business for his stable of lawyers to handle was to be successful over the long haul, not only new clients, but a constant flow of new legal talent would be needed to replenish the natural losses. Young blood, that was Adelbert Fleischmann and Al Mugel's specialty. Mugel was in a position to see and judge the best talent in the region through his teaching position at one of the nation's finest law schools. Adelbert often did the hiring, in many cases adding the tender loving care needed to keep competing high-powered egos in check.

Few associates ever made partner without substantial contributions to the firm but as the Jaeckle Fleischmann team passed its half century mark in 2005, a number of partners were remembered in death for their unique personalities and contributions. Each was a part of what had become the Jaeckle Fleischmann aura.

John M. Montfort

John Montfort had a totally unobtrusive personality that served him well as the quiet, thoughtful counselor to major clients, and as managing partner of a growing firm for a period of nearly ten years in the 1970s. Adelbert Fleischmann recalls the 35-year-old Montfort coming to the firm after the death of his father, Stanley, in the mid 1960s. Stanley Montfort and his wife headed up a husband-wife-son legal team that specialized in corporate law and estate planning. The Montforts had some pretty high-level clients but upon the death of his parents, John Montfort recognized a need for the resources of a larger firm. [12]

The Newman family, the Cowpers, and the Anderson family were just some of the names associated with the Montforts. The Newmans distributed and sold gasoline and petroleum products all across Western New York under the Ashland name. In more recent years, their neat green and white NOCO stations have become a fixture in upstate New York. The Cowper construction business acted as general contractor at major construction sites all over the area. Large Cowper construction signs at building sites made their family name famous. The A.E. Anderson family never had the name recognition of the Newmans and NOCO in Western New York, but their Anco company, based in Buffalo, gained a worldwide reputation for rebuilding and relining blast furnaces, a high-stakes specialty that went unnoticed as long as it was carried out correctly. John Montfort was counselor to these families, as well as to the Middle Atlantic Warehouse Distributors which began as a small auto parts cooperative in Buffalo and grew into one of the top ten auto parts companies in the nation. John was known as a solutions man who developed a close relationship with his clients, and 15 years after his death, Tom Palmer, Jean Powers, Tim Loftis and Peter Klein were among those at Jaeckle Fleischmann still servicing clients introduced to the firm by Montfort.

The Montforts were a Buffalo family and John attended Canisius High School and Canisius College before earning his law degree from Cornell University in 1954. John was known as a devoted family man who liked to have his lunch at the Buffalo Athletic Club, but he often was not part of the late night or weekend talk-fests in the office or the downtown clubs. He and his wife, the former Sheila Stein, raised three sons and a daughter in their Snyder home.

John was described by colleagues as a "fantastic managing partner" who could synthesize very complex issues and come out with a reasoned judgment.

To the youngest associates, he was a manager who could instill fear in you as he carefully took notes in his short yellow pad with an oversized fountain pen. It all depended on where you stood. But even a young Ed Piwowarczyk, who saw him as the representative of the power of Ed Jaeckle during his firm manager years, was fast to add that if John recognized you as a valuable prospect, he would protect and insulate you. "If I needed a role model," said Piwowarczyk, "John would have been my role model in every way."

One Saturday morning in July 1990, John played his usual tennis match with one of his sons and then went home to take a mid-day nap. He was found dead 20 minutes later. He was only 61 years old. He had suffered from severe asthma. Once when he was asked why he didn't move his family to Arizona and practice, he answered matter-of-factly: "I don't have any clients in Arizona." [13]

Lawrence H. Wagner

Larry Wagner was the gentleman litigator who never spiced his language with obscenities and never erupted in anger, but if you were in trouble, he was the go-to guy. Adelbert Fleischmann recruited Larry from public service and the Fleischmann and the Wagner families remained friends throughout their lives. Wagner was a good-faith skeptic, always meticulous in his preparation and precise in his questioning. In his quiet, intellectual way, when he cross examined witnesses, they didn't survive. He was elected a fellow in the American Society of Trial Lawyers, the highest honor a trial lawyer can attain. Manly Fleischmann and Harry Kelly had held that honor and John Stenger would attain the distinction later.

Wagner grew up on Lemon Street but he was a generation younger than Ed Jaeckle. He attended St. Louis Parish School, Canisius High School, Holy Cross College and earned his law degree from UB in 1949, after an interruption caused by World War II. He worked for the state attorney general in various capacities for 10 years in Albany and Buffalo, during which time he was involved in the condemnation of properties along the path of the State Thruway. [14] After joining Jaeckle Fleischmann in the late 1950s, Wagner represented companies whose land was being condemned for the Kensington Expressway. He represented Mount Calvary Cemetery, the largest cemetery in Western New York. Within the cemetery association, he took some good-natured ribbing as the guy who caused Mount Calvary to lose its magnificent granite gates when the expressway carved a path right through the heart of the cemetery, including the site of the Pine Ridge Road gates. But to be sure, the state did so for a price. And later, when there was a growing controversy over cemetery liability in headstone vandalism, Larry Wagner is the one who drafted suggested legislation which became the law of the state just as he wrote it.

Wagner always found time to mentor young lawyers and Michele Heffernan recalls sitting with Jean Powers on the lounge chair in Wagner's office well past 7 o'clock in the evening, taking in every word from the senior counselor. Probably no one gained more from Wagner's sharing of his experience than Howard S. Rosenhoch, a 1976 graduate of the UB Law School who developed a long friendship with the older Wagner.

Larry Wagner retired at the age of 77 in early 2003 as chairman of the firm's litigation section. He was honored as the Erie County Bar Association's Lawyer of the Year in 2003, and he died Jan. 30, 2005.

John G. Putnam Jr.

"A tidy ship is a happy ship," was one of the favorite adages of John Graves Putnam Jr., a man who spent his entire 47-year legal career with Jaeckle Fleischmann. A Navy veteran and a captain in the Naval Reserve, Putnam was known to sneak obvious quick looks at his wristwatch at meetings during his three years as managing partner. That usually meant the meeting was either over or it should be.

Putnam was hired by Adelbert Fleischmann upon his graduation from the UB Law School in 1957. He headed up the firm's estates practice and specialized in trusts, working closely with Al Mugel. John was a member of a prominent Buffalo family. His great-grandfather had served in government under Abraham Lincoln. His family tree could be traced back to Gen. Israel Putnam, a hero of the Battle of Bunker Hill and George Washington's second-in-command on Long Island, where Gen. Putnam, a Connecticut Yankee, would play a pivotal role in the evacuation of the Continental Army in the face of overwhelming British forces. [15]

As a member of the Naval Reserve for 35 years, John Putnam regularly sang the National Anthem before the Buffalo Sabres hockey games. Putnam was especially proud of appearing on the 50-yard line in full Naval uniform to sing the National Anthem before a Buffalo Bills game as part of Armed Forces weekend at a packed Ralph Wilson Stadium.

Putnam grew up on Lancaster Avenue and graduated from Nichols and Duke University before attending law school at UB, where he was a Mugel tax student. He married Thekla Polley during his last year at law school, and he clerked for Jaeckle Fleischmann that year in the Rand Building offices. Putnam had started singing in the choir at St. John's-Grace Episcopal Church when he was seven years old and he continued singing in that choir for nearly 70 years. He was an avid tennis, squash and bridge player, but Thekla revealed she didn't like being his bridge partner. "He was a perfectionist and he questioned everyone's moves." He became dean of the Saturn Club, his favorite place to dine out, and was president of the Buffalo Tennis and Squash Club.

After his death at 76 on Nov. 9, 2005, his colleague Gayle Eagen sang a song in his memory at the firm's 2005 Christmas Party. James Tanous recalled that this many-faceted man had played baseball with Yankee great Bobbie Richardson as an undergraduate at Duke.

John H. Stenger

If one were writing a novel and the protagonist were a big-time commercial litigator, you would write the story of John Stenger. When he walked into a room he looked and acted like a litigator. When you got into an argument with him, he just wore you down. When he was involved in a case, he was committed and impassioned and he poured every fiber of his being into his case. You might think he wondered how the world continued to revolve outside of his case. [16] A darling of the local media, Stenger was involved in some of the most celebrated local cases of the second half of the 20th Century. He represented clients in the Love Canal environmental disaster, the Attica Prison riot fallout and multiple First Amendment cases for *The Buffalo News* and the local television outlets. But the case that consumed nearly 20 years of his life was the notorious Domed Stadium case.

In the mid-1960s, Buffalo auto dealer Edward H. Cottrell proposed building a domed stadium home for the Buffalo Bills on an 800-acre site he had assembled in the Town of Lancaster. Bills Owner Ralph C. Wilson was threatening to move his team because of an inadequate stadium in the city. *The Buffalo Evening News*, spearheaded by editor Paul E. Neville, was championing the Lancaster site and the rival *Courier-Express*, under Executive Editor Douglas

Turner, was pushing just as hard for a Downtown Buffalo location. Erie County was to build the facility, the centerpiece for a much larger Cottrell enterprise. After months of acrimonious debate in the County Legislature, and preliminary votes both up and down, the legislators approved, and Erie County signed, a contract for the $50 million Domed Stadium. Site work began but before the first concrete was poured, the county reneged on its contract, claiming the initial bids were too high, and eventually it built an open-air stadium at a compromise site along Abbott Road in Orchard Park.

What ensued was a $495 million breach of contract suit against the county that pitted two legal heavyweights, Victor T. Fuzak for businessman Cottrell and John Stenger, special counsel for Erie County. It was a court-watchers delight. Fuzak of the Hodgson Russ firm and Stenger of Jaeckle Fleischmann. Stenger who graduated from Kensington High School, Canisius College and was first in his class at the UB Law School in 1958, and Fuzak, who attended Bennett High School, Williams College and the Harvard Law School, would fight over this case from 1971 until June 1989 when the State Court of Appeals refused to consider any more arguments in the case. Fuzak initially bested Stenger in 1984, winning a jury judgment of $62 million for his client. The Appellate Division upheld that decision. But by the summer of 1989, when the state's highest court heard the last appeal, the judgment against the county had been whittled down to about $10 million, including accrued interest. Of the unending litigation, *Buffalo News* columnist Ray Hill wrote: "People who watch leave with the sense that they have seen perfection, or something close to it." [17]

In 1993, the flamboyant Stenger, along with a few other attorneys, left Jaeckle Fleischmann and formed Stenger & Finnerty. Despite some bruised feelings at 12 Fountain Plaza when Jaeckle Fleischmann first learned of the move from clients while Stenger was vacationing out of town, Adelbert Fleischmann counted Stenger as a friend until his death. "I miss John," said Adelbert. "I used to have lunch with him almost every week, even after he left us. He was president of the Buffalo Club and we used to like to eat over there. We remained good friends."

Stenger died March 30, 2002, leaving his wife of 49 years, the former Janet Liebler, three daughters and three sons.

Another Stenger "career case," one stemming from the 1971 riots at the sprawling Attica State Correction Facility 30 miles east of Buffalo, stretched on for nearly three decades. It would be January 2000 before another Jaeckle Fleischmann litigator, Mitchell J. Banas Jr., would participate in a case-closing settlement.

The Attica Prison riot began on Thursday, Sept. 9, 1971, under a cloud of disputed reports of torture, prisoner mistreatment, racism and severe over-crowding at the maximum security facility in Wyoming County. The rioting received national media attention as it escalated over the next 24 hours. Several guards were beaten, one of them fatally, and the rioting prisoners killed two or three fellow prisoners in what was termed "prison justice." More than a thou-sand inmates took control of a major portion of the facility and held hostage 40 guards and civilian employees. On Monday, Sept. 13, after more than two days of failed negotiations, much of it played out on nightly television news, Gov. Nelson Rockefeller, who had presidential aspirations, authorized the retaking of Attica by whatever means necessary. It was a decision that would plague Rockefeller for the rest of his life.

A State Police helicopter, under the ultimate command of State Police Major John Monahan, dropped tear gas over D-Yard, opening the bloodiest prison assault in modern American history. In six minutes of lethal gunfire from police rifles and shotguns, 29 inmates and ten hostages died, and another 89 were injured. [19]

Decades of criminal and civil litigation would follow and John Stenger would be in the midst of it, representing State Corrections Commissioner Russell G. Oswald. Civil lawsuits were filed in 1974 on the eve of the statute of limitations, but then the cases went dormant for nearly 15 years. In the late 1980s, a class-action suit was brought on behalf of the 1284 inmates in D-Yard against various state officials. Mitch Banas was among those assisting Stenger in the defense of Commissioner Oswald.

In the Spring of 1992, nearly 20 years after the riots, Oswald was exonerated of one charge and the jury was hung on a second charge. Of all the defendants, the only defendant with a verdict against him was a local mid-level prison man-ager, deputy assistant superintendent Karl Pfeil.

After two separate damage trials, juries brought back damages against Pfeil of $3 million for Frank (Big Black) Smith, one of the ringleaders in the upris-ing, and $75,000 for a relatively unknown inmate named David Brosig. Given the most conservative figures, extrapolated over the 1284 inmates included in the class action, the state liability could easily have reached $100 million.

Through a variety of circumstances, including Stenger's leaving the Jaeckle firm and the retirement of Pfeil's attorney, Mitch Banas inherited the verdicts. Banas and his colleagues took the liability and individual damages verdicts to the Second Circuit Court of Appeals which reversed the liability determination. Then, in January 2000, 29 years after the riot, attorneys for all parties reached an $8 million settlement, with most inmates, or relatives of inmates, to receive just $6,500 each. [20]

J. Edmund DeCastro Jr.

Jed DeCastro was a free-spirited litigator who claimed family ancestry back to the Mayflower, but also claimed affinity to the city's Hispanic minority. One colleague said you never knew whether he was representing an Hispanic small business owner from the West Side or whether he had just taken a millionaire client to visit a major shipbuilder. Besides his usual negligence cases, DeCastro had a special interest and expertise in Admiralty Law. He was a lieutenant commander in the Naval Reserve and could be seen chomping a cigar in his dress whites during the summer months.

DeCastro graduated from the UB Law School in 1953 and joined Jaeckle Fleischmann in 1957, after serving as a gunnery and fire control officer aboard the heavy cruiser USS Toledo in the Korean War. DeCastro came from a seagoing family that included three generations of naval officers. He was a president of the local Naval Reserve Association and a commodore of the Buffalo Yacht Club. He founded the Buffalo Maritime Heritage Foundation and was responsible for a series of visits to Buffalo by sailing ships and war vessels in the 1970s. Jed DeCastro is remembered for arranging the visit to Buffalo of the Norwegian square-rigger, the Christian Radich, in 1976 as part of the bicentennial celebration. Thousands of persons from all over the Northeast visited the ship docked at Buffalo Harbor. [21]

A Buffalo native and graduate of Canisius High School and Canisius College, DeCastro, after 35 years at Jaeckle Fleischmann, opened his own office in 1994. He died Oct. 19, 2003.

Brian J. Troy

Brian Troy was a brilliant fun-loving guy who could be abrasive and aggressive while being a very effective litigator and labor and employment attorney. One of his best friends and colleagues, who described him as a great lawyer and a great friend, was known to refer to Troy as Brian-the-Pain. A debonair fellow, Troy was a man about town. Troy met and married the 1972 Miss Buffalo, Norma Alesii, and the couple became a fixture at Buffalo social events. [22]

A native of New York City, Troy earned his law degree from UB and worked briefly for Jaeckle Fleischmann in the late 1960s, was recruited as confidential law clerk to Federal Judge John O. Henderson, and then returned to Jaeckle Fleischmann in 1972. The Troys were world travelers and for a time, they maintained a second home in Italy. Brian had a passion for professional sports, sports cars, fishing and gourmet cooking. What many didn't know about Troy, was that he gave countless hours of his time to the United Cerebral Palsy Association, Opportunities Unlimited and the Legal Aid Bureau. [23]

Troy underwent heart surgery while in his mid-50s and never fully recovered, although he returned to work for a time. Norma died in 1999, and a year later, Brian died at age 57.

William Schapiro and Other Modern Leaders

The so-called Founding Fathers, a tight-knit group whose makeup varied over the years but always included Ed Jaeckle and Manly and Adelbert Fleischmann, exercised a strong influence over the firm, but they never mired themselves in its day-to-day administrative detail. Over the years, the task of managing a firm that at times has totaled around 90 persons, fell to an elected firm manager or managing partner, or in most recent years, a combination executive committee chairman and firm manager.

The contributions of staff managers like Dwight Campbell, Joseph Swart, John Montfort, John Putnam and Timothy Leixner already have been documented, but in the firm's more recent history, with the Founding Fathers' oversight a thing of the past, the task of managing the firm has taken on added significance.

For example, William I. Schapiro held the top chair on the executive committee under various titles for more than 15 years starting in 1985 and in the words of more than one colleague: "Bill Schapiro *was* Jaeckle Fleischmann for a very long period."

These were years of both growth and change as Buffalo went through a period of transformation away from heavy industry. And during that time, Schapiro, a Wesleyan University and Harvard Law School graduate, also represented two nationally prominent real estate investment trusts and was principal outside counsel for Seneca Foods, currently the largest vegetable canner in the world.

A native of Newark, N.J., Schapiro credits his moving to Buffalo to his wife, the former Susan Rubenstein of Buffalo whom he met at Harvard, and his joining the Jaeckle Fleischmann firm in 1965 to Al Mugel. Schapiro recalls Ed Jaeckle advising him to look for clients among the up and coming, the action-oriented people.

One of the firm's notable successes in that regard is the approximately 30-year relationship it has maintained with two clients headquartered in Jackson, Ms., EastGroup Properties, Inc., and Parkway Properties, Inc., both of which are real estate investment trusts, generally referred to as REITs in the financial world.

Partner Joseph Kubarek, who handles these two REITs today, recalled that they had been Jaeckle Fleischmann clients since before he arrived in 1983. "Bill Schapiro made the original client contacts," he said. "Bill handled them during their development years and it was Bill and Jim Tanous who actually developed that niche business for us."

The "niche business" today consists of two REITS traded on the New York Stock Exchange that have real estate holdings valued in the hundreds of millions of dollars each.

Bill Schapiro, after nearly 15 years of managing the Jaeckle Fleischmann firm, was characterized by his colleagues as the glue that holds the place together, the peacekeeper, and one of the smartest persons in the firm. [24]

Later, Thomas A. Palmer, who has been engaged in general corporate, merger and acquisition, and financing and tax for 26 years, was managing partner for about seven years. Palmer had been a CPA before joining Jaeckle Fleischmann and most recently has worked out of the firm's Amherst Office.

"In this business, there's nothing wrong with your driving force being survival," said James Tanous, who was chairman of the Executive Committee from 2002 until 2007. "The business today is different from anything I was prepared for in law school." Tanous is a native of Olean and a graduate of St. Bonaventure

University and the University of Virginia Law School. As a partner in the firm's business and corporate practice group, he represented U.S. and international publicly traded companies. He was a director of the Erie, Pa.-based insurer, the Erie Insurance Group, and in the Spring of 2007, Tanous was named that company's executive vice president, corporate secretary and chief lawyer. He left Jaeckle Fleischmann at the end of April 2007 and relocated to Erie.

Tanous worked closely with managing partner Edward G. Piwowarczyk who succeeded him as Executive Committee chairman and continued to hold the title of managing partner. Piwowarczyk originally aspired to being a poverty lawyer doing legal aid work in his native Lackawanna. A graduate of UB and the John Marshall Law School in Chicago, Piwowarczyk joined Jaeckle Fleischmann in 1972. He left to head up labor relations for Erie County during a portion of the Ned Regan and Ed Rutkowski administrations before returning to private practice and then returning to Jaeckle Fleischmann about 1983.

A partner in the firm's labor and employment practice group, Piwowarczyk specializes in management labor relations law and public employment relations law. In that role, he was instrumental in negotiating a master agreement that would help facilitate the merger of Buffalo General, Children's, Millard Fillmore Gates, Millard Fillmore Suburban and DeGraff Memorial, along with their ancillaries, into what would become known as Kaleida Health, a hospital corporation that in the late 1990s employed more than 4,000 health care workers in Western New York.

By 2007, Piwowarczyk estimated his duties as chairman and managing partner were filling about 80 percent of his work day. [25] Managing the firm, with a total staff of nearly 100 persons in several locations, had come a long way from the days of Dwight Campbell, when according to Adelbert Fleischmann, "Ed Jaeckle was in charge, no question about it."

CHAPTER VIII

Epilogue

By the winter of 1977, Manly Fleischmann, at an age when many Americans are thinking of retirement, still was enjoying his grueling weekly commute to Webster & Sheffield in New York. On this particular week in late January, he had met his brother Adelbert, Paul Weaver and J.B. Walsh for a meeting of the state Bar Association. American Airlines notified Manly, by now a 20-year director of the company, that despite perfect flying weather in New York, it was snowing in Buffalo and the forecast called for a lot more. American suggested his group catch an earlier flight, probably the last one that would fly back to Buffalo that day.

When the four men got off the plane in Buffalo, it was snowing indeed, and high winds were blowing the nearly 30 inches of accumulated snow, some of which had fallen as early as Christmas, but never melted. Briefcases in hand, with no overshoes, they made their way to Manly's car and it was decided Adelbert would drive, drop his older brother at home, and bring the rest of the group to the office in the Liberty Bank Building. The going was slow and a treacherous wind was causing those notorious Buffalo whiteouts along the Kensington Expressway. Some cars were off the road. By the time they reached Oakland Place, drifting snow was up to a man's thigh and the street was impassable, so they decided to let Manly walk the half block from Summer Street. He would tell his colleagues later that the only thing that got him home was the thought of the next day's newspaper headline: Prominent Lawyer Found Frozen on Oakland Place. [1]

From there, it was back to the office for the rest of the group. Adelbert, finding many of his staff stranded downtown, sent across Main Street to AM&As department store for blankets, and a large number of Jaeckle Fleischmann lawyers and staff did what thousands of other Buffalo residents did during the first night of the Blizzard of '77. They settled down in front of television sets and watched an episode of Alex Haley's *Roots*, and then spent the night down-town.

By this time, Manly was recognized as one of the top litigators in the nation. Unlike Ed Jaeckle, you didn't see him walking around the offices at Jaeckle Fleischmann, making small talk with the young associates. Manly was far from prim and proper, but he never mastered the art of chit-chat. He was a genuine person, not above an occasional off-color story, but he could be a little bit of an intellectual snob. He didn't suffer fools gladly is how his colleagues put it. He didn't waste his time on people he didn't consider very bright. That was Manly, for good or for bad. [2] He liked an intellectual challenge and he relished work. Paul Weaver recalled leaving the office many a night after 9 o'clock, and seeing Manly Fleischmann still behind his desk. For Manly and many of the partners and young associates, Saturdays were a highlight of the week. That's the day everyone broke for lunch and headed to the Tap Room at the Lafayette Hotel to take part in – or just listen to – legal discussions into late afternoon. Ed Piwowarczyk said the discussions sometimes were over his head, and for a Genesee beer-drinker from Lackawanna, the martinis were a test of his man-hood. On the few occasions a year when Fleischmann broke his routine, he and Lois would fly to Canada or Maine for the quiet excitement of a salmon stream.

He remained close to the arts. He was a life trustee of the Buffalo Philharmonic Orchestra and a director of the Albright-Knox Art Gallery. He also was instrumental with Gov. Nelson Rockefeller in the founding of Artpark in Niagara County, although the lion's share of the credit for building that summer arts facility in Lewiston goes to state Senate Majority Leader Earl W. Brydges. His son, Thomas E. Brydges, and Michele Heffernan were on the Artpark board for several years, with Heffernan remaining active at Artpark to this day. Tom Brydges, a graduate of Syracuse University, joined the firm in 1973 and is a partner in the firm's labor and employment group.

Colleagues Odza and Halpern recall the day earlier in the decade when Manly Fleischmann and his historic rival Frank G. Raichle argued the case over the not-for-profit status of the Cornell Aeronautical Laboratory before the State Appellate Division. Odza recalls that John Stenger was "carrying Manly's briefcase and I was carrying John's briefcase." Ralph Halpern was carrying Frank Raichle's briefcase. A high-level attorney in State Atty. Gen. Louis Lefkowitz's office represented the state and carried his own briefcase. Before the opening of arguments, the chief judge of the Appellate Division noted for the record how honored the court was to have before it both Manly Fleischmann and Frank Raichle. "If that didn't make the poor assistant attorney general feel like second fiddle," commented Odza. [3]

Then, one day in 1980, the firm learned that Manly Fleischmann had suffered a mild stroke while having dinner with Lois and friends at the Buffalo Club. He was in Buffalo General Hospital but the prognosis was good and he would be back to work in a month or so. He returned home but didn't seem to be recovering. When his wife and daughter accompanied him to Massachusetts General Hospital for further treatment, and after visits by his brother Adelbert and Al Mugel, it became apparent that the "mild stroke" had been a serious medical event.

Manly Fleischmann's New York commutes were over. He remained active in the firm and his office was maintained, but his trips downtown were irregular and his colleagues noted he was not the same Manly Fleischmann. In the summer of 1983, Manly and Lois celebrated their 50th wedding anniversary at the Buffalo Club. During the years after his initial stroke, he received numerous honors, including the Distinguished Citizen Award of the State University in 1982, and the 1983 Red Jacket Award for long-term public service to the Historical Society. He already had received UB's highest award, the Chancellor Norton Medal. [4]

On March 25, 1987, Manly Fleischmann collapsed in his Oakland Place home while discussing Jaeckle Fleischmann business with his best friend, Adelbert. He died in an ambulance on the way to Millard Fillmore Hospital.

Manly Fleischmann had talked of the eventuality of death with his daughter, granting the need for a funeral service at St. Paul's Cathedral "for your mother," even though he claimed he never liked "the preacher man," his generic term for the clergy. And there would be a "top-drawer party." It didn't turn out exactly as planned. There was a big funeral, with eulogies by several old friends, burial in the cathedral crypt and a party at Alison's Irving Place home. But more than a dozen friends from Webster & Sheffield, who had chartered a plane for the trip to Buffalo, were left on the LaGuardia runway because of bad weather in New York. [5]

In his eulogy, Al Mugel said of his friend: "Manly was sometimes impatient, but never intolerant, and always understanding, and extended his help beyond ordinary measure." And then Mugel added: "At heart, he was an adventurer. I recall him standing on the prow of a ferry boat crossing a sound and suddenly saying to me: 'I would have liked to have been an explorer.'" [6]

Six weeks later, a memorial service was held in the Church of the Heavenly Rest at Fifth Avenue and 91st Street in Manhattan. It had been arranged by colleagues at Webster & Sheffield, and Ethan A. Hitchcock, another long-time friend, spoke. Hitchcock said that despite Manly's customary three-day week in New York, he was a "full time, hugely respected and beloved partner." Then he quipped: "Lois used jokingly to complain that her husband was the only lawyer she knew who couldn't earn a living in one city." [7]

Fleischmann had once told the trustees of the State University, when he was trying to have a new UB Law School building named after his friend, John Lord O'Brian, who was still living at 97: "When you deserve an honor and you're 97, the difference between that and being dead is very small." The trustees broke policy against naming buildings for living persons and named the building for O'Brian who died the following year. [8]

Manly Fleischmann had been much honored in life but his greatest interests in life had been education, the arts, and most of all, the law, and the law firm he would leave as his legacy. It is fitting that in his death, the law firm would found, sponsor and support the Bennett High School Law Magnet, an award winning example of public education in Buffalo, coordinated in recent years by partner Heath J. Szymczak.

* * *

Over the years, Adelbert Fleischmann had developed a long and genuine friendship with Ed Jaeckle. It was not unusual to see Adelbert and his wife Helen with Jaeckle and Grace at the Buffalo Club, or at the Park Lane Restaurant in the building below the Jaeckles's Park Lane apartment, or at their favorite country spot, the Old Orchard Inn in East Aurora. Jaeckle often talked politics, but by his own choice, he was out of the circle. He meant it when he said that politics and a law practice didn't mix. He confided to colleague Odza that Nelson Rockefeller had asked him to come out of political retirement and become state GOP chairman to cleanse the state party during the L. Judson Morehouse scandal, but on this occasion, Jaeckle turned down his good friend. [9]

At times, it became Adelbert's job to enforce the firm's no-politics rule. Adelbert recalled how back in 1970 he counseled a bright, young associate named John J. LaFalce to leave the firm and make a run for the State Senate. John was hoping for a leave of absence or a guarantee that he could return. "Life is short," Adelbert told the young associate. "If you really want to get into politics, go for it." [10] John, a Canisius College and Villanova University graduate, won the seat and was elected to the State Assembly two years later. Then in 1974, he was elected to the U.S. House of Representatives, where he served 28 years before retiring from Congress in 2003. When he retired, he was ranking member on the Committee on Banking and Financial Services. "He had a pretty good run for it," Fleischmann said of LaFalce. The two remained good friends.

Another young lawyer who left the firm to make a name elsewhere was David Fielding, who in the mid-1960s become general counsel for Roblin Industries, where Michele Heffernan recalls working with him years later on employee benefits.

But the granddaddy of those who got away was Ralph Halpern who described himself as the associate who took the longest to make partner at Jaeckle Fleischmann. Halpern left as an associate in 1957 to go with the Raichle firm. Twenty-eight years later, he returned to Jaeckle Fleischmann and became a partner. Halpern also was late getting his undergraduate degree. After World War II, he was a math major at UB but he is said to have gotten itchy to start a career so he jumped over to the Law School where he graduated summa cum laude. After Halpern, the Law School insisted on an undergraduate degree for admittance so he was the last UB Law School graduate without a bachelor's degree. More than 50 years later, two days after his 77th birthday, Halpern donned cap and gown and walked across the UB stage to receive his undergraduate degree. [11]

* * *

Ed Jaeckle never lost his love for communicating with the staff. He had lunches at the Park Lane for younger staff members, dinners at the Buffalo Club, or he just dropped in on someone to discuss a case. Michele Heffernan remembers the breezy "Good morning counselor" in the Fountain Plaza elevator.

And Alison Fleischmann recalls decades earlier being greeted with: "Well hello little lady." Both knew that this was Jaeckle's way of covering up for not remembering their names. Jim Tanous talks of the always impeccably dressed Jaeckle walking into his office in shirt sleeves, wearing his starched white shirt, a tie and his gold cufflinks. He could have used the telephone to get the information he sought but Ed Jaeckle was a man with the personal touch.

Paul Weaver remembers the day he was paired with Jaeckle at the Country Club of Buffalo. "He wasn't bad at golf. He was shooting in the 90s when he was 70 years old." On this day, a young associate was playing in the foursome in front of Jaeckle, and was having a difficult go of it. Finally, Jaeckle turned to Weaver and asked: "Is he any good?" When Weaver said the young man was very bright and a promising litigator, Jaeckle quipped: "Well that's good because he sure as hell can't play golf." [12]

On another day, Weaver was working late and heard his boss's distinctive nasal voice at the door: "Mr. Weaver, I want you to meet a good friend of mine." Weaver looked up to see Jaeckle entering his cubicle with Richard Nixon. Nixon was a former vice president at that time but had not yet been elected president. Weaver recalls that Jaeckle liked to walk around the office and introduce his friends to the staff. There was never any question that he was proud of his stable of partners and associates.

In May 1976, Jaeckle's wife of more than 50 years, the former Grace Dreschel from the Fruit Belt and his constant companion for a lifetime, died after a long illness. The Jaeckles had left for Florida each year right after Christmas and the following Christmas, almost out of habit, Ed Jaeckle got on the plane alone and headed for St. Petersburg. His associates felt a little sad for him. He returned shortly after New Year's and to the receptionist's friendly "Welcome back. How was Florida," he answered: "Just fine. Well, I got married." It took 30 seconds for that news to be relayed to every office in the firm. [13]

Jaeckle married Erma R. Hallett, a lawyer and widow from Buffalo who had been practicing in St. Petersburg. The wedding was a quiet afternoon service at St. Peter's Episcopal Cathedral in St. Petersburg. When asked his new wife's age, he would only say: "Everyone knows I'm 82." [14] Years later, Erma Jaeckle said she was 63 when they were wed. "No one was more surprised than I when he said he wanted to marry me." [15]

The couple came back to Buffalo and maintained homes in the Park Lane

Apartments and in Florida. They traveled extensively for the next decade, including cruises on the Mediterranean and the Adriatic. Mrs. Jaeckle was living in St. Petersburg in 2007.

Odza recalled an incident in Fountain Plaza which epitomized the Jaeckle character. A blind beggar, well known to the Main Street crowd, had made his way up the elevator to see Jaeckle. An associate was trying to dissuade the disheveled and somewhat malodorous man from approaching the reception desk but the receptionist intervened. She recognized him. She called Jaeckle who came out, gave the man a bear hug and took him back to his office where they chatted for nearly an hour. Later Jaeckle explained to Odza that the beggar had been a classmate of his at Masten Park High School and was down on his luck. The two visited twice a year, once in Buffalo and once in Florida. "He had no airs about him. He was a social animal. He loved people," recalled Odza.

Another time, during the Watergate scandal, Judge John J. Sirica showed up at the annual Gridiron Dinner in Washington and saw Jaeckle in the crowd. "He walked over, threw his arms around me and introduced me to everybody as an important guy," Jaeckle told a reporter. "I finally recalled why he remembered me. He was one of the speakers at Shea's Buffalo during the Wendell Willkie campaign in 1940." [16]

In the mid 1980s, Jaeckle was struck by a car on an icy Court Street and when a partner suggested he would ride in the ambulance to Buffalo General Hospital with Jaeckle, the boss urged him to go back to work. It is said he conducted a meeting from his bed at Buffalo General in his starched white shirt, a tie and his gold cufflinks. In the late '80s, Jaeckle fell and broke his leg on the concrete stairs leading down to Huron Street from Fountain Plaza. Weaver recalls that his recovery was slower this time, but after a time on a walker and then a cane, the 90-year-old Jaeckle was back walking the halls of Jaeckle Fleischmann.

Then in 1988, to everyone's surprise, Ed Jaeckle announced that he would retire, sell his Buffalo apartment and limousine and move to Florida. Ed and Erma spent a short time living in an apartment near the Mayo Clinic in Rochester, Minn., and then moved to Florida. Suffering from terminal cancer, he stayed in touch with the office in Buffalo for the next three years from Florida.

Edwin F. Jaeckle died on May 14, 1992, in St. Petersburg at the age of 97.

A memorial service was held a week later at St. Paul's Cathedral in Buffalo and his ashes were interred in Forest Lawn Cemetery. At the memorial service, his long-time friend Ruppert Warren said:

> "Integrity was a byword with Ed. Integrity was the very foundation of his long political career, during which there was never the slightest suggestion of personal profit to him. ... He was interested only in good, honest government and that is what he got because he would not tolerate anything else. ...

> "As a lawyer, Ed's ethics were impeccable. He would neither cross the line nor continue to work for a client who asked him to. ...

> "In closing, I want to mention Ed's congeniality, conviviality and pure love of living. In any group of which he was a part, there was never a dull moment." [17]

Appendix I – Genealogy

Jaeckle Fleischmann & Mugel
(1971-72 to Present)

Wilcox & Van Allen merger with no name change
(1956-57)

Jaeckle, Fleischmann, Kelly, Swart & Augspurger
(1955 to 1971-72)

Fleischmann, Augspurger, Campbell & Mugel
(1954)

Fleischmann, Augspurger & Campbell
(1953-1954)

Cohen, Fleischmann, Augspurger, Henderson & Campbell
(1952-1953)

Fleischmann, Augspurger, Henderson & Campbell
(1949-1952)

Fleischmann & Augspurger
(1945 to 1949)

Fleischmann Brothers
(Pre-World War II)

Williams, Marion & Fleischmann
(After 1933)

Garono, Jaeckle, Kelly & Swart
(1953-55)

Garono, Jaeckle, Kelly & Wick
(1952-1953)

Garono, Jaeckle & Kelly
(Circa. 1940s)

Ladd, Garono & Jaeckle
(Circa. 1930s)

Palmer, Garono, Houck & Wickser
(Circa. 1920s)

Schelling & Garono
(Jaeckle admitted to bar in 1915)

Robert F. Schelling
(Jaeckle clerked for Schelling before 1915)

Note: Chronology is based on 1974 chronology prepared by Michele Heffernan, Thomas Brydges and James Tanous on the occasion of Jaeckle's 80th birthday. Dates are from sometimes conflicting newspaper and magazine articles.

Appendix II: Highlights of the Jaeckle Political Career

1916 – Jaeckle wins a seat on the Board of Supervisors from the old 11th Ward.

1918 – Jaeckle wins re-election but resigns in January 1919 to accept the position of clerk of the Board of Supervisors.

1926 – Jaeckle wins a seat on the State Republican Committee.

1928 – Jaeckle named Erie County collector of back taxes.

1935 – Jaeckle is elected Erie County Republican chairman.

1937 – Jaeckle runs for mayor of Buffalo and loses to Thomas F. Holling by 1,427 votes.

1938 – Jaeckle leads a group of GOP reformers in nominating Thomas E. Dewey for governor in an unsuccessful attempt to win the statehouse.

1940 – Jaeckle is elected New York State Republican chairman, controlling the largest bloc of delegates at national conventions.

Jaeckle heads unsuccessful campaign to win the presidential nomination for Dewey. Wendell Willkie is his party's nominee and Willkie loses to incumbent President Roosevelt.

1942 – Dewey wins the governorship and Jaeckle is put in charge of shepherding Dewey's legislative agenda.

1944 – Jaeckle leads drive for Dewey presidential nomination by acclamation at Chicago convention. Dewey loses wartime election to incumbent FDR.

Jaeckle quits as state GOP chairman 10 days after the Dewey election defeat.

1947 – Dewey and Jaeckle reconcile as Dewey eyes another run at the White House.

1948 – Jaeckle accompanies Dewey on the campaign train throughout the Fall, but in November, Dewey is upset by Truman.

Shortly after the election, Jaeckle retires from politics and devotes full-time to his Buffalo law practice.

Appendix III

[The following OpEd article written by Manly Fleischmann was published Jan. 8, 1973, by the New York Times. The date of publication is noteworthy in that many of the same questions discussed in the Fleischmann Commission's report are being debated in the year 2007. The article is reprinted as it appeared, with permission of the New York Times Inc.]

The Education of Manly Fleischmann

By Manly Fleischmann

When Governor Rockefeller and the State Board of Regents invited me in October of 1969 to head a special commission whose task was to find out how New York State might get better public education for less money, my first reaction was a mixture of surprise and disbelief.

Surprise, because I had not even heard of the creation of the commission, although it had been set up and funded by the Legislature earlier that year. Disbelief, because I had no track record of any kind in the subject matter of the proposed investigation.

But Governor Rockefeller is a persuasive man, and a few days later I accepted the invitation, principally because he replied to my protestations of lack of expertise by reminding me of Clemenceau's observation that "war is much too serious a matter to be entrusted to the military."

Today New York State is poorer by almost $2-million, the amount invested in the work of the Commission on the Quality, Cost and Financing of Elementary and Secondary Education, as our group was impressively and ambitiously titled by the Legislature. We like to believe New York is richer by three bulky volumes of what the commission and its staff intended to be the most intensive investigation of public education ever undertaken by a single state.

We hope, but are not yet sure, that the commission's report will affect education in New York State importantly. Whatever the ultimate effect of our work, however, it has certainly had a deeply educational impact on the members of the commission, most of whom (like the chairman) had little reliable knowledge of educational problems when the work began.

For me, at least, these were three years of learning and, often more importantly, unlearning; of becoming acquainted with a vast field of knowledge and theory which had been a closed book to me; of thinking through and sometimes discarding instinctive beliefs which I had long held without ever appraising their validity; of coming to understand what Justice Holmes meant when he pointed out that "Time has upset many fighting faiths." I propose to summarize these educational experiences in a few of the thousand and one matters we had to consider.

1. **The State of Education**. To our surprise, we discovered – and the discovery was repeated time and again in the course of our study – that there was no agreed upon body of goals, principles or practice in our system of public education. Perhaps it should not be so surprising that there is disagreement about the goals of education, since different families want different things for their children. But it did come as a shock to many of us to learn, for example, that after thousands of years of effort there was still wide disagreement on such an elementary matter as the best method of teaching children to read. Here, the proponents of at least five

different "systems" urged their respective merits with all the zeal characteristic of what I referred to above as a "fighting faith."

2. Causes of Educational Failure and Suggested Remedies. No educational controversy is more current or more confused than this. I was alarmed, however, to discover that New York State – as well as many other states – is encountering an unacceptably high rate of student failure, particularly in the acquisition of the three skills most essential to an effective adult life — reading, writing and arithmetic. The schools tend to be least productive in low-income areas, both urban and rural, but it is also typically the case that less money is spent per pupil in these same areas. Those who believe there is truth in the maxim that you get what you pay for would attempt to redistribute educational funds on the basis of educational need.

3. Financing Public Education. In 1969 I dwelt in an almost total state of ignorance as to how public education was financed. Three years have changed all that; and to paraphrase a currently popular author, I have since been exposed to more than I ever wanted to know about educational financing. In the course of this painful process, many of my beliefs were discovered to have no validity.

I suppose my most shocking discovery in this area was the unfairness of the manner in which educational revenues are raised, and the greater inequity of the system under which these revenues are allocated. In my innocence, I had supposed that revenues were of necessity raised largely on the basis of ability to pay, and that distribution was on the basis of educational need.

It never occurred to me that it would be possible in an enlightened state for affluent families to pay less in taxes for the education of their children than their lower-income neighbors in a nearby district, while at the same time the children of the latter families had about half as much public money spent on their education as did the children of the richer families.

We soon came to see that this basic infirmity in the financing of public education was the central problem which had to be solved before substantial progress could be made in other areas; we therefore proposed state assumption of education costs and far-reaching changes in distribution of resources.

John Gardner, we think, put it correctly when he said in effect: "Every discussion of public education must necessarily commence and conclude with the subject of money."

4. The Education of Children with Special Needs. I had considered myself a reasonably informed citizen, but I simply could not have been made to believe that more than half of our identifiably handicapped children in New York State receive no special education of any kind. Neither did it seem possible that tens of thousands of non-English speaking children would be expected to learn in a classroom presided over by a teacher who spoke only English – but these are the sorry facts.

5. Accountability. As an individual who had devoted a few years of his life to public service, I was perhaps less impressed than many citizens by the continuous protest of taxpayers' groups against what they thought of as the indefensible waste of money in the educational system. It soon became apparent, however, that many of their charges were justified.

We concluded that education is being underfinanced, but that much of the needed additional expenditure could be eliminated if the public insisted on getting its money's worth.

It was shocking, for instance, to learn that the need for additional school space was invariably met by a proposal to build a new school building, while legislation designed to permit use of the buildings throughout the year was successively defeated by two sessions of the Legislature.

Similarly, we learned that New York State had a higher percentage of administrative officials, as compared with teachers, than any other state of the union. Further, many of us learned for the first time that an incredible situation had developed involving excessive pension arrangements for teachers, and that this situation threatened the future financial integrity of the state and particularly New York City. Some of our recommendations dealt with these questions.

Accountability, like motherhood, is a term that enjoys universal approval; the difficulty is that no one can agree as to just what accountability means in an educational system. We concluded, however, that it is not impossible to devise a system of performance accountability, and we made proposals designed to put our feet securely on that road.

6. Technology. At the outset of our study I shared with many others an almost mystic confidence in the potential of the technology of the computer world to correct the defects and control the costs in our educational system.

That confidence still persists, but now I realize regretfully that the realization of that potential is still a long way off, largely because the cost of development is staggering. Since the cost would be prohibitive to any single state and the fallout from development would benefit every state, we urged that the Federal Government bear such costs.

7. Integration — A Lost Hope? In this area I was subjected to a wholly different and painful kind of learning process during my years on the commission. Like so many other Americans, I completely misjudged the temper of the American people and the calculated purpose of the Nixon Administration to halt and then to reverse the steady progress of racial integration in the public schools in the South while simultaneously undermining efforts to check the trend toward increased segregation in the North. It soon became evident that Northern de facto segregationists were at least as heartless and determined as their Southern de jure counterparts.

8. The Future of Education In New York State. In one broad area of concern our surprises were fewer and more pleasant. We had believed in a general way that despite its faults the New York education system was on the whole as good as any in the country, and clearly better than most. Judging from what comparisons we could make, this proved to be the fact.

When we consider the inadequacies of our educational system, it is a distressing commentary on the state of education elsewhere in the United States that this is true.

While New York's problems are many, pervasive and frightening, it is my own belief that the faith of the American people in public education is on the whole justified and that no investment of public funds appears to offer equal promise for the future of our great democracy.

Mr. Fleischmann, a Buffalo Lawyer, was chairman of the New York State Commission on the Quality, Cost and Financing of Elementary and Secondary Education.

Appendix IV: Partners, August 2007

Joseph W. Allen – Admitted to practice in 1990; educated at Hamilton College (B.A., cum laude, 1986), State University of New York at Buffalo (J.D., 1989), note and comment editor of *Buffalo Law Review*. Allen is administrator of the firm's litigation practice group; specializes in bankruptcy law, creditors' rights, commercial law and litigation and ERISA litigation. He has lectured on bankruptcy litigation and creditors' rights. He is moderator of the WNY Bankruptcy Conference and is chairman of the Erie County Bar Association's Commercial and Bankruptcy Law Committee.

Mitchell J. Banas Jr. – Admitted to practice in 1986; educated at State University of New York at Fredonia (B.A., cum laude, 1982), Grove City College, State University of New York at Buffalo (J.D., cum laude, 1985), executive editor of *Buffalo Law Review*. Banas has extensive experience in complex tort and commercial litigation; specializes in trial and appellate practice, complex litigation, construction law, insurance law and business litigation. He is a past treasurer of the WNY Trial Lawyers Association.

Paul A. Battaglia – Admitted to practice in 1973; educated at Canisius College (B.S., 1969), State University of New York at Buffalo (J.D., magna cum laude, 1972), research editor of *Buffalo Law Review*. Battaglia is a partner in the firm's tax practice group; specializes in taxation, tax exempt organizations, estate planning, corporate tax planning and international taxation. He is adjunct professor at the UB Law School and has been an instructor and lecturer at Canisius, UB and the Erie County Bar Association.

Sean P. Beiter – Admitted to practice in 1992; educated at Canisius College (B.A., magna cum laude, 1988), State University of New York at Buffalo (J.D., cum laude, 1991), article editor of *Buffalo Law Review*. Beiter is administrator of the firm's labor and employment practice group; specializes in management labor relations law, labor arbitration, public employment relations law, public and private sector collective bargaining, employment-at-will. He has lectured in business and labor forums and is active in Boy Scouts.

George F. Bellows – Admitted to practice in 1986; educated at Hamilton College (A.B., 1974), Syracuse University (M.B.A., 1980), State University of New York at Buffalo (J.D., cum laude, 1985), publications editor, *Buffalo Law Review*. Bellows is a partner in the firm's business and corporate and financial services practice groups; specializes in banking law, financing transactions law and corporate law. He is an officer in the Buffalo Council of World Affairs and a director of the Elmwood-Franklin School.

Kristen M. Birmingham – Admitted to practice in 1998; educated at Franklin & Marshall College (B.A., cum laude, 1994), Syracuse University (J.D., cum laude, 1997), associate editor, *Syracuse Law Review*. Birmingham is a partner in the firm's business and corporate law, and securities law practice groups. Birmingham was made partner in 2007.

David G. Brock – Admitted to practice in 1973; educated at Union College (B.A., 1967), State University of New York at Buffalo (J.D., 1972). Brock is a partner in the firm's litigation practice group; specializes in negligence, personal injury, product liability, insurance coverage and litigation, trial practice and appeals. He is an author and journal editor, and has lectured and been an instructor at Emory University Law School and the UB Law Convocation. He has been an officer of Planned Parenthood of Buffalo and Erie County and is past president of Temple Beth Zion.

Thomas E. Brydges – Admitted to practice in 1974; educated at Syracuse University (B.A., cum laude, 1971, J.D., 1973), Phi Delta Phi. Brydges is a partner in the firm's labor and employment practice group; specializes in management labor law, college law, business immigration law, affirmative action and OSHA. He is a decorated Army veteran of Vietnam. He is a lecturer and adviser in higher education, and is a current or past officer or director of Daemen College, Artpark, the Theodore Roosevelt Inaugural Site Foundation and the Buffalo Niagara Youth Chorus.

B. Kevin Burke, Jr. – Admitted to practice in 2000; educated at Georgetown University (B.A., cum laude, 1995), George Washington University (J.D., 1999). Burke is a partner in the firm's litigation practice group and has been a presenter for the National Business Institute. He is a board member of Child & Family Services Annual Giving Foundation. He was made a partner in 2007.

Dennis B. Danella – Admitted to practice in 2000; educated at Clarkson University (B.S., with distinction, 1997), University of Kansas (J.D., 2000). Danella is a patent attorney and a partner in the firm's intellectual property practice group; specializes in patent, copyright and trademark, trade secret and trade dress law. He has worked with a variety of technologies, including fuel cells, vehicle valve actuation systems, fire and water-resistant containers and others. He was made partner in 2007.

Victoria L. D'Angelo – Admitted to practice in 1979; educated at State University of New York at Buffalo (B.A., 1973), New York Law Clerkship Program. D'Angelo is a partner in the firm's estates and trusts practice group, specializing in estate and trust planning and administration and elder law. She has been an instructor at Medaille College and has served as justice for the Village of Williamsville. She was made partner in 2007.

Michael C. Donlon – Admitted to practice in 2000; educated at St. Bonaventure University (B.B.A., summa cum laude, 1995), State University of New York at Buffalo (J.D., magna cum laude, 1999), note and comment editor, *Buffalo Law Review*. Donlon is a partner in the firm's corporate law and corporate governance practice groups; specializes in representing public and private companies in connection with securities offerings, mergers and acquisitions, corporate governance, securities regulation and general corporate matters. He was made partner in 2007.

Gayle L. Eagan – Admitted to practice in 1986; educated at Medaille College (B.A., 1966), Canisius College (M.S., 1977), State University of New York at Buffalo (J.D., cum laude, 1985). Eagen is a partner in the firm's estate and trusts practice group; specializes in estate planning, trust and estate administration and litigation, Article 81 guardianships and elder law. She is current or past president of Estate Analysts of Western New York, National Academy of Elder Law, Legal Services for the Elderly of Western New York, and an officer of the Community Foundation of Greater Buffalo.

Patrick L. Emmerling – Admitted to practice in 1994; educated at Canisius College (B.S., summa cum laude, 1984), University of Notre Dame (J.D., magna cum laude, 1993). Emmerling is a partner in the firm's estates and trusts practice group; specializes in estates and trusts, federal gift and estate taxation law and elder law. He has been an adjunct professor at Canisius College and is an officer of the Financial Planning Counselors of WNY.

J. Montieth Estes – Admitted to practice in 1970; educated at Cornell University (B.Ch.E., 1965; M.Ch.E, 1966), Harvard University (J.D., 1969). Estes is managing partner of the firm's Rochester Office and administrator of the firm's intellectual property practice group, and a partner in the firm's business, corporate, intellectual property and emerging company practice groups; specializes in business and corporate law, intellectual property, venture capital financing law, technology and science and emerging company law. Estes has represented and held executive positions in a host of start-ups in New York and Florida, and is experienced in fund raising, executive recruiting, technical hiring and running companies.

Charles D. Grieco – Admitted to practice in 1996; educated at Colgate University (B.A., summa cum laude, 1989), Columbia University (M.A., 1992), State University of New York at Buffalo (J.D., summa cum laude, 1995), executive editor, *Buffalo Law Review*. Grieco is a partner in the firm's environmental and economic and land development practice groups and specializes in environmental litigation and environmental compliance. He has been a director and officer of the New Millennium Group of WNY.

Ralph L. Halpern – Admitted to practice in 1953; educated at the University of Buffalo (J.D., cum laude, 1953), associate editor, *Buffalo Law Review*. Awarded undergraduate degree from State University of New York at Buffalo at age 77 in 2006. Halpern is a partner in the firm's business and corporate, financial services and international trade practice groups; specializes in corporate law, antitrust law, defamation law, legal ethics and discipline law, sports law, litigation and appellate practice. He has been a teacher and lecturer, and has been president of the Buffalo Council of World Affairs, Temple Beth Zion and Bureau of Jewish Education of Greater Buffalo, and an officer or director of the Buffalo Chapter American Jewish Committee and the Jewish Federation of Greater Buffalo.

Vincent O. Hanley – Admitted to practice in 1983; educated at the State University of New York at Oswego (B.A., cum laude, 1979), State University of New York at Buffalo (J.D., cum laude, 1982). Hanley is a partner in the firm's business and corporate, economic and land development, financial services, and real estate practice groups; specializes in real estate, commercial law, financing, foreclosure law, lease law, real estate taxation, zoning and planning and environmental law. He is a director of Hilbert College and the St. Vincent DePaul Society.

Dennis P. Harkawik – Admitted to practice in 1980; educated at New York University School of Engineering (B.Ch.E., 1972, M.Ch.E., 1974), New York University School of Public Administration (M.P.A., 1974), State University of New York at Buffalo (J.D., cum laude, 1979), articles editor, *Buffalo Law Review*. Harkawik is administrator of the firm's environmental practice group, chairs the firm's economic and land development practice group, and is a member of the firm's international business practice group; specializes in environmental law, public utility law and administrative law.

Michele O. Heffernan – Admitted to practice in 1975; educated at the College of New Rochelle (B.A., 1971), State University of New York at Buffalo (J.D., cum laude, 1974), managing editor, *Buffalo Law Review*. Heffernan is a member of the firm's employee benefits practice group; specializes in ERISA and employee benefits, including pension, profit sharing, 401 (k), employee stock ownership, stock options and various other compensation plans. She is a member and a past chairman of Artpark and past chairman of the Holy Angeles Academy Board of Trustees.

Brenda J. Joyce – Admitted to practice in 1987; educated at the State University of New York at Buffalo (B.S., magna cum laude, 1983, J.D., magna cum laude, 1986), publications editor, *Buffalo Law Review*. Joyce is a partner in the firm's environmental practice group; specializes in environmental law, including the state Environmental Quality Review Act, compliance counseling, enforcement proceedings, Superfund litigation, and solid and hazardous waste regulation. She is a frequent speaker at bar association functions and for private organizations.

Daniel P. Joyce – Admitted to practice in 1984; educated at Notre Dame University (B.A., 1976), State University of New York at Buffalo (M.B.A., with distinction, 1984, J.D., magna cum laude, 1984), book review editor, *Buffalo Law Review*. Joyce concentrates his practice on business, immigration and cross-border matters and is a partner in the firm's intellectual property group; specializes in business and corporate law, immigration, intellectual property and transportation law. He is a teacher, lecturer, author and regular columnist in trucking periodicals.

Ronald J. Kisicki – Admitted to practice in 1986; educated at Western Michigan University (B.S., 1970), Rochester Institute of Technology (M.B.A., 1976), Detroit College of Law (J.D., cum laude, 1986). Kisicki concentrates on intellectual property law, litigation and emerging company law; specializes in intellectual property litigation, including patent, trademark/trade dress, copyright and trade secrets, patent interference, patent prosecution, patent portfolio management and emerging company law. He is a past member of the editorial board of the Syracuse Business Journal's international business publication.

Peter G. Klein – Admitted to practice in 1980; educated at State University of New York at Buffalo (B.A., magna cum laude, 1976), Albany Law School of Union University (J.D., cum laude, 1979), note and comment editor, *Albany Law Review*. Klein is administrator of the firm's business and corporate practice group; specializes in a wide variety of business transactions, including acquisitions, divestitures, business restructuring, financing transactions, contract and business enterprise matters, export regulation and health care. He is a member and former chairman of the American Heart Association's WNY Regional Advisory Board.

John T. Kolaga – Admitted to practice in 1986; educated at Canisius College (B.A., 1982), State University of New York at Buffalo (J.D., 1985), articles editor, *Buffalo Law Review*. Kolaga is a partner in the firm's environmental practice group; specializes in environmental law, environmental litigation, general civil litigation and municipal law. He is a director and past president of Brush Up Buffalo, director and past chairman of the Niagara Frontier Section, Air & Waste management Association, past vice president of the Parish Council at the Buffalo State College Newman Center.

Joseph P. Kubarek – Admitted to practice in 1983; educated at the University of Rochester (B.A., cum laude with high distinction, 1979), Northwestern University (J.D., 1982), note and comment editor, *Journal of Criminal Law and Criminology*. Kubarek is a partner in the firm's business and corporate practice; specializes in corporate law, securities law, securities offerings, venture capital law, mergers and acquisitions. A significant portion of his practice involves representing real estate investment trusts. He has been an adjunct professor at the UB Law School.

Anthony J. Latona – Admitted to practice in 1972; educated at Canisius College (B.S., 1969), State University of New York at Buffalo (J.D., 1972). Latona is a partner in the firm's litigation practice group; specializes in business disputes, complex commercial litigation, dispute resolution of development issues, construction law, product liability law and personal injury litigation. He has lectured widely and has been an instructor at Canisius and adjunct instructor at Daemen College. He has been a director of the Amherst Chamber of Commerce, Youth Leadership of Erie County and the Amherst Symphony Orchestra.

Tim C. Loftis – Admitted to practice in 1981; educated at the State University of New York at Buffalo (B.A., magna cum laude, 1976), Georgetown University (J.D., cum laude, 1980). Loftis is a partner in the firm's business and corporate practice group; specializes in mergers and acquisitions, business law, corporate law and franchise law. His experience includes general counsel for a large regional food distributor and franchiser. He is an officer and director of the Buffalo Niagara Partnership.

Katherine H. McGuire – Admitted to practice in 1989; educated at State University of New York at Binghamton (B.S., 1987), Franklin Pierce Law Center (J.D., 1989), University of Rochester (M.S., currently enrolled). McGuire is a partner in the firm's intellectual property and emerging company practice groups; specializes in negotiating and preparing agreements relating to intellectual property, including IP license, technical service, confidentiality and consulting. She was made a partner in 2007.

John M. Monahan – Admitted to practice in 1997; educated at Hobart College (B.A., with high honors, 1991), George Mason University (J.D., 1996), editor-in-chief, *George Mason University Civil Rights Law Journal*. Monahan is a partner in the firm's labor and employment practice group; specializes in labor and employment litigation, covenants-not-to-compete, civil litigation, employment discrimination law, human resources and management consulting. He was made partner in 2007.

Randall M. Odza – Admitted to practice in 1967; educated at Cornell University College of Industrial and Labor Relations (B.S., 1964), Cornell Law School (L.L.B., 1967), editorial board and business manager, *Cornell Law Review*. Odza is a partner in the firm's labor and employment practice group; specializes in labor management law, anti-discrimination, employer-employee relations, private and public sector bargaining, public sector labor and employment law, job safety and health law and wage and hour law. He is an officer and board member of the Buffalo Philharmonic Orchestra, and was chairman of the orchestra's *Carnegie Express* Event Committee.

Thomas A. Palmer – Admitted to practice in 1975; educated at Canisius College (B.S., 1970), State University of New York at Buffalo (M.B.A., 1971, J.D., magna cum laude, 1975). Palmer practices in the firm's corporate practice group; specializes in corporate and partnership law, acquisitions, divestitures and mergers, joint ventures, bank and venture capital financing, health care law, taxation, emerging company law, corporate governance, debt and equity financing. He holds numerous titles in the UB School of Management, is a member of the Catholic Diocese Committee for Education Awards, and is a founding member of the Minority and Women Emerging Entrepreneur Program.

Robert W. Patterson – Admitted to practice in 1984; educated at the State University of New York at Buffalo (B.A., summa cum laude, 1980; J.D., magna cum laude, 1983). Patterson concentrates his practice on employee benefits, estates and tax practice groups; specializes in ERISA, qualified retirement plans, executive compensation and welfare plans. He advises business with regard to benefit plan issues relating to mergers and acquisitions.

Michael A. Piette – Admitted to practice in 1981; educated at the State University of New York at Buffalo (B.A., cum laude, 1977; J.D., 1980). Piette is a member of the firm's real estate practice group; specializes in commercial and residential real estate, real estate finance, commercial leasing and title insurance law. He has been a director of leadership Niagara, a member of Niagara Falls and Niagara County commissions and a director of Family and Children's Service of Niagara.

Edward G. Piwowarczyk – Admitted to practice in 1971; educated at State University of New York at Buffalo (B.A., 1968), John Marshall Law School (J.D., with honors, 1971). Piwowarczyk is the firm's chairman and managing partner and is a partner in the firm's labor and employment practice group; specializes in management labor relations law, public employment relations law, public sector collective bargaining, municipal law, educational law. He formerly was director of labor relations for Erie County. He is a former president of the NYS Employers Labor Relations Association, the Advocates Society of WNY, the Organization of Public Employer Negotiations of WNY, and the Employee Relations Officers – NYS Association of Counties.

Jean C. Powers – Admitted to practice in 1980; educated at St. John's University (B.A., cum laude, 1968; M.A., 1971), State University of New York at Buffalo (J.D., magna cum laude, 1979), research editor, *Buffalo Law Review*. Powers is a partner in the firm's real estate practice group, specializing in commercial real estate, real estate finance, commercial leasing, title insurance law and title opinion law. She is a past president of the UB Law Alumni Association, a trustee of Trocaire College, a trustee of the University at Buffalo Foundation, a past president of Volunteer Lawyers Project, an executive board member of the National Association of Women Business Owners, and is active in a wide variety of community and educational associations.

Raymond P. Reichert – Admitted to practice in 1980; educated at Fordham University (B.A., magna cum laude, in cursu honorum, 1976), State University of New York at Buffalo (J.D., cum laude, 1979). Reichert is a partner in the firm's tax practice group; specializes in federal and state taxation, partnership taxation, real estate investment trusts, mergers and acquisitions, low income housing and historic tax credits. He has been an adjunct assistant professor at the UB Law School. He is a director of the Oncologic Foundation of Buffalo, Legal Aid Bureau, and WNY Independent Living Project.

Steven J. Ricca – Admitted to practice in 1988; educated at the University of Michigan (B.A., high honors, 1984), State University of New York at Buffalo (J.D., cum laude, 1987), member, *Buffalo Law Review*. Ricca is a partner in the firm's environmental and economic and land development practice groups; specializes in environmental and land use litigation, environmental review procedures and regulatory compliance. He is a committee chairman of the Buffalo Olmsted Parks Conservancy and a past officer of the Food Shuttle of WNY.

Howard S. Rosenhoch – Admitted to practice in 1977; educated at the State University of New York at Buffalo (B.A., 1971), Hunter College, City University of New York (M.A., 1973), State University of New York at Buffalo (J.D., cum laude, 1976). Rosenhoch is a partner in the firm's litigation practice group; specializes in civil trials, appeals, product liability law, insurance coverage, professional malpractice law and real estate litigation. He was confidential clerk to Justice Jeremiah J. Moriarty. He is a past president and board member of Hillel of Buffalo, and a board member of the Jewish Federation of Greater Buffalo and Temple Beth Zion.

Dennis K. Schaeffer – Admitted to practice in 2000; educated at Boston College (B.A., summa cum laude, 1993); State University of New York at Buffalo (J.D., magna cum laude, 1999), assistant executive editor, *Buffalo Law Review*. Schaeffer is a partner in the firm's litigation practice group; specializes in complex litigation, commercial law and litigation and ERISA litigation. He is a tutor in Bennett High School's Law Magnet Program. He was made partner in 2007.

William I. Schapiro – Admitted to practice in 1957; educated at Wesleyan University (B.S., with high distinction, 1951), Harvard University (J.D., 1954). Schapiro is a partner in the firm's business and corporate practice group; specializes in corporate law, corporate financing law, securities and venture capital law and mergers and acquisitions. He was chairman of the firm's executive committee for more than a decade. Schapiro is a former Assistant U.S. Attorney for the Western District of New York. He has been active in a variety of community activities, including many years as a trustee or director of the University at Buffalo Foundation. He was a lecturer on corporate law and commercial law subjects at the UB Law School.

Andrew O. Scheinman, Ph.D. – Admitted to practice in 2002; educated at the University of Illinois (B.S., 1982), University of California at Los Angeles (Ph.D., 1989), California Western School of Law (J.D., 1998). Scheinman is a partner in the firm's intellectual property practice group; specializes in biotechnology, intellectual property, patent law and emerging company law. He has done post- doctoral research in biotechnology at UCLA and has published bioethics and biotechnology studies in scientific journals. Prior to joining the firm, he drafted key SARS patents for the Chinese National Human Genome Center and the Harbin Veterinary Research Institute.

Charles C. Swanekamp – Admitted to practice in 1980; educated at Northwestern University (B.A., 1976), State University of New York at Buffalo (J.D., 1979; M.B.A.,

1980). Swanekamp is a partner in the firm's litigation practice group; specializes in general contract and commercial disputes, corporate, environmental and intellectual property litigation, sports law, securities law, antitrust, and accountant professional responsibility. He maintains a practice in sports law, counseling amateur and professional athletes. He is president of the UB Alumni Association.

Heath J. Szymczak – Admitted to practice in 1999; educated at Canisius College (B.S., summa cum laude, 1994; M.B.A., cum laude, 1995), State University of New York at Buffalo (J.D., 1998), business editor, *Buffalo Law Review*. Szymczak has a general litigation practice with a concentration in business-related and commercial litigation. He was confidential law clerk to Judge William M. Skretny. He is active in student mentoring at the UB Law School and works with students at Bennett High School. He is vice president and a director of Buffalo Alliance for Education.

Nicole R. Tzetzo – Admitted to practice in New York State and U.S. Tax Court; educated at Xavier University (B.S./B.A., cum laude, 1995), Catholic University of America (J.D., 1998). Tzetzo is administrator of the firm's Employee Benefits, Estates and Tax practice groups, and is a partner in the firm's business and corporate, and emerging company practice groups; specializes in tax and business matters, including corporation and partner formation, mergers and acquisitions, debt and equity financing and contract matters. She was made partner in 2007.

Matthew C. Van Vessem – Admitted to practice in 2000; educated at State University of New York at Buffalo (B.A., magna cum laude, 1992; J.D., 1997). Van Vessem is a partner in the firm's labor and employment practice group; specializes in labor and employment matters, public sector collective bargaining, civil service law and municipal law. He formerly was assistant corporation counsel for the City of Buffalo. He was made partner in 2007.

Paul C. Weaver – Admitted to practice in 1961; educated at Canisius College (B.S., 1958) University of Buffalo (L.L.B., 1961, J.D., 1965), editor, *Buffalo Law Review*. Weaver is a partner in the firm's business and corporate practice group; specializes in business and corporate law and health care. He is a past president of the UB Law School Alumni Association, a past president of the Erie County Bar Association and the Bar Foundation, and active in the state Bar Association. He is a past chairman of the Hilbert College trustees and a recipient of its President's Medal. He is a director of Mercy Flight, a vice chairman of the United Way of Buffalo & Erie County and active in the Studio Arena and Catholic Charities appeals.

Sources

Richard Norton Smith, *Thomas E. Dewey and His Times*, Simon & Schuster, 1982

Murray B. Light, *From Butler to Buffett*, Prometheus Press, 2004

Buffalo and Erie County Historical Society Archives, unpublished papers of Alfred H. Kirchhofer

The Autobiography of Emanuel Fleischmann

Unpublished remarks of Frank C. Moore at Oct. 27, 1964, testimonial for Jaeckle

The UB Law Forum, Edwin Jaeckle Edition, 1986

Unpublished Biography: Edwin F. Jaeckle Center for State and Local Democracy,
   State University of New York at Buffalo Law School

C. Eugene Miller, *Gothic Grandeur*, Canisius College Press, 2003

James Napora, *Houses of Worship*, unpublished master of architecture thesis

"The Rockefellers," *American Experience*, PBS-WGBH, Boston

Nancy Isenberg, *Fallen Founders*, Viking Press, 2007

Newspapers and Periodicals:

Buffalo Business
Buffalo Law Journal
The Buffalo Courier-Express
The Buffalo Evening News
The Buffalo News
The Buffalo Times
The Chicago Tribune
Harper's Magazine
Living Prime Time (Buffalo, N.Y.)
The New York Times
Time Magazine
The Washington Post

Interviews with founding Jaeckle Fleischmann partners:

Adelbert Fleischmann, April 3, 2006, and April 10, 2006
J.B. Walsh, Sept. 7, 2006
John Wick, Sept. 28, 2006

Interviews with current Jaeckle Fleischmann partners:

Mitchell J. Banas Jr., March 26, 2007
J. Montieth Estes, March 19, 2007
Ralph Halpern, May 10, 2006
Michele Heffernan, June 16, 2006
Joseph P. Kubarek, March 13, 2007
Randall Odza, May 4, 2006, and Dec. 1, 2006
Edward Piwowarczyk, June 20, 2006, and April 12, 2007.
William Schapiro, April 28, 2006
Heath J. Szymczak, March 12, 2007
Paul Weaver, May 16, 2006

Other Interviews:

George Borrelli, retired political reporter, *The Buffalo News*, July 13, 2006.
Alison Fleischmann, daughter of Manly Fleischmann, Sept. 19, 2006
Erma R. Hallett Jaeckle, Edwin Jaeckle's second wife, July 28, 2006.
Monsignor James Kelly, son of Harry Kelly, Sept. 8, 2006.

Tim Leixner, former partner, now of Florida, Sept. 25, 2006
Richard Mugel, son of Albert Mugel, Sept. 14, 2006
Thekla Putnam, wife of John G. Putnam Jr., Sept. 12, 2006.
Michael Swart, son of Joseph Swart, Sept. 13, 2006.
James Tanous, former partner and Executive Board chairman, June 6, 2006
Anne (Wagner) Tierney, daughter of Lawrence Wagner, Sept. 7, 2006.
Douglas Turner, Washington Bureau chief, *The Buffalo News*.

Footnotes

Chapter I
Introduction: The Firm with Three Unpronounceable Names

1. The lyrics were found in 1974 in a file marked "1958 – Jack Mimmack" at the firm offices.
2. The Fleischmann quote is from an interview with Michele O. Heffernan, June 16, 2006.
3. The *Washington Post*, Aug. 7, 1954.
4. The characterization of Fleischmann is from "Truman's Guns-and-Butter Man,"
   by Robert J. Donovan, *Harper's Magazine*, January, 1952.

Chapter II
Edwin F. Jaeckle: From Humble Beginnings

1. *Houses of Worship*, James Napora, unpublished master of architecture thesis.
2. *The Buffalo News Magazine*, March 2, 1980.
3. Interview with Ralph L. Halpern, May 10, 2006.
4. Ed Jaeckle Profile, Bob Watson, *Buffalo Business*, August 1963.
5. *UB Law Forum*, author anonymous, Winter/Spring 1986.
6. *From Gothic Grandeur*, C. Eugene Miller, Ph.D., Canisius College Press, 2003.
7. Interview with John Wick, Sept. 28, 2006.
8. *The Buffalo Evening News*, Feb. 18, 1948.
9. *The Buffalo News Magazine*, March 2, 1980.
10. *Buffalo News* biographical files from 1953.
11. *The Buffalo Evening News*, May 17, 1976.
12. Unpublished remarks of Frank C. Moore at a testimonial dinner for Jaeckle, Oct. 27, 1964.
13. *The Buffalo Evening News*, Feb. 18, 1948.
14. Ibid.
15. *The Buffalo Times*, Sept. 24, 1935.
16. Ibid.
17. The *New York Times*, Dec. 29, 1935.
18. *The Buffalo News Magazine*, March 2, 1980, quoting a Buffalo Times reporter.
19. *Buffalo Magazine*, "Man of the Year," by Paul Jayes, January, 1974.
20. The *New York Times*, Dec. 27, 1935.
21. Ibid., Jan. 7, 1936 and Jan. 9, 1936 stories.
22. Ibid., April 17, 1936.
23. Ibid., May 9, 1937.
24. Ed Jaeckle Profile, Bob Watson, Buffalo Business, August 1963.
25. Interview with William I. Schapiro, April 28, 2006.
26. Interview with George Borrelli, July 13, 2006.

Chapter III
The Fleischmann Brothers: Designed for Success

1. The opening narrative uses a combination of materials from "Truman's Guns-and-Butter Man," by
   Robert J. Donovan, *Harper's Magazine*, January, 1952, and interviews with Adelbert Fleischmann,
   April 3 and April 10, 2006.
2. *The Autobiography of Emanuel Fleischmann*, completed February, 1901, privately printed
   December, 1973.

3. *The Buffalo Evening News*, Dec. 7, 1951.
4. *The Buffalo Evening News*, Feb. 23, 1952.
5. Ibid.
6. *The Autobiography of Emanuel Fleischmann.*
7. *Harper's Magazine*, January, 1952.
8. Interviews with Adelbert Fleischmann.
9. Ibid.
10. Ibid.
11. Interview with Alison Fleischmann, Sept. 19, 2006.
12. *Harper's Magazine*, January, 1952.
13. Ibid.
14. "The World of Manly Fleischmann," by Anthony Cardinale, *The Buffalo News Magazine*, July 8, 1979.
15. Manley's one dip into politics is a combination of "The World of Manly Fleischmann," interviews with Adelbert Fleischmann, an interview with Mrs. John G. Putnam Jr., Sept. 12, 2006, and *Harper's Magazine*, January, 1952.
16. Interview with Alison Fleischmann.
17. Interview with Adelbert Fleischmann.
18. *Harper's Magazine*, January, 1952.
19. Interview with Adelbert Fleischmann.
20. "Three in Law Firm Vets of World War II," by H. Katherine Smith, *Buffalo Courier-Express*, Oct. 20, 1946.
21. Interview with Adelbert Fleischmann.
22. Interview with Alison Fleischmann.
23. *Buffalo Courier-Express*, Oct. 20, 1946.
24. Interviews with Adelbert Fleischmann and *Buffalo Courier-Express*, Oct. 20, 1946.
25. *Buffalo Courier-Express*, Oct. 20, 1946.

Chapter IV
Jaeckle: Ten Years in the National Spotlight

1. *New York Times*, Sept. 30, 1938.
2. *Thomas E. Dewey and His Times*, Richard Norton Smith, Simon & Schuster, New York, 1982, p.266 (Hereafter referred to as Smith's *Dewey*).
3. The first reference by Jack Meddoff in *The Buffalo Evening News*, Feb. 18,1948; the *New York Times* obituary, May 16, 1992.
4. Smith's *Dewey*, p.272.
5. *Washington Post*, April 14, 1940.
6. Smith's *Dewey*, p.30.
7. Ibid., p.264.   (The Jaeckle description appeared in *Time Magazine, The Buffalo News* several times, *The New York Times*, and undoubtedly other publications.)
8. Ibid., p.19.
9. *New York Times*, April 13, 1940.
10. The unpublished papers of Alfred H. Kirchhofer, Buffalo & Erie County Historical Society, June 2, 1939 (Hereafter referred to as Kirchhofer Papers).
11. Smith's *Dewey*, pp.309-314.
12. Kirchhofer Papers, Oct. 2, 1940.
13. Smith's *Dewey*, p.304.
14. Ibid., p.345.
15. Kirchhofer Papers, Nov. 4, 1942.
16. *New York Times*, May 23, 1943.
17. Unpublished transcript of remarks by Frank C. Moore, files of Jaeckle Fleischmann & Mugel.
18. *The Buffalo News Magazine*, March 2, 1980.
19. Interview with William I. Schapiro, April 28, 2006.
20. Smith's *Dewey*, p.398.
21. Kirchhofer Papers, Dec. 9, 1943 and Dec. 11, 1943.
22. *Time Magazine*, May 29, 1944.
23. *Washington Post*, June 26, 1944.

24. *New York Times*, June 30, 1944.
25. Smith's *Dewey*, p.405.
26. The incident was recounted by several sources; the Jaeckle reaction is from a Jaeckle interview for Smith's Dewey, p.408.
27. Interview with Randall M. Odza, May 4, 2006.
28. *The Buffalo News Magazine*, May 2, 1980.
29. Interview with Erma Hallett Jaeckle, July 28, 2006.
30. *New York Times*, Nov. 16, 1944.
31. *New York Times Sunday Magazine*, Sept. 12, 1948.
32. The incidents are from *The Buffalo Evening News*, Feb. 18, 1948 and *The Buffalo News Sunday Magazine*, May 2, 1980.
33. Smith's *Dewey*, p.481.
34. *Time Magazine*, July 5, 1948.
35. *Washington Post*, Sept. 13, 1948.
36. Interview with Randall M. Odza.
37. Smith's *Dewey*, p.515.
38. Opposing accounts are from *The Buffalo Evening News*, Oct. 12, 1974, and Smith's *Dewey*, p.538.
39. Interview with William I. Schapiro.
40. Interviews with Ralph L. Halpern, May 10, 2006 and Paul C. Weaver, May 16, 2006.
41. *The Buffalo Evening News*, Nov. 4, 1938.
42. Interview with Randall M. Odza.

Chapter V
Manly Fleischmann: A Star on the National Stage

1. Interview with Alison Fleischmann, Sept. 19, 2006.
2. The *Buffalo Courier-Express*, Sept. 30, 1950.
3. Press Release from the United States Department of Commerce, dated Jan. 24, 1951, under the name of Secretary Charles Sawyer, from the archives of *The Buffalo News*.
4. "Truman's Guns-and-Butter Man," by Robert J. Donovan, *Harper's Magazine*, January, 1952.
5. Ibid.
6. *The New York Times*, July 24, 1951.
7. *Harper's Magazine*, January, 1952.
8. *Time Magazine*, Nov. 27, 1950.
9. *Time Magazine*, July 9, 1951.
10. Interview with Alison Fleischmann.
11. *Harper's Magazine*, January, 1952.
12. The Churchill visit is a combination of accounts from the interview with Alison Fleischmann and "The World of Manly Fleischmann," by Anthony Cardinale, *The Buffalo News Magazine*, July 8, 1979.
13. From the Fleischmann family scrapbook, with permission of Alison Fleischmann.
14. The *Washington Post*, May 8, 1952.
15. *The Buffalo News Magazine*, July 8, 1979.
16. Interview with Randall M. Odza, May 4, 2006.
17. Rockefeller's announcement is a combination of The New York Times, Oct. 29, 1969 and *The Buffalo Evening News*, Sept. 2, 1972.
18. The *New York Times*, Feb. 18, 1963 and May 24, 1964.
19. Interview with William I. Schapiro, April 28, 2006, and interview with Alison Fleischmann.
20. The *New York Times*, Jan. 29, 1972.
21. The *New York Times*, Feb. 10, 1972.
22. *Times Magazine*, Feb. 7, 1972.
23. *The Buffalo Evening News*, editorials of Jan. 31, 1972 and July 17, 1972.
24. The *New York Times*, Jan. 10, 1973.
25. *The Buffalo Evening News*, Sept. 2, 1972.
26. "The Education of Manly Fleischmann," by Manly Fleischmann, The *New York Times*, Jan. 8, 1973.
27. Interview with Randall M. Odza.

28. The *New York Times*, March 27, 1987.
29. Interview with William I. Schapiro.

Chapter VI
The Group of 13: The Founding Partners

1. Interview with J.B. Walsh, Sept. 7, 2006.
2. Interview with Adelbert Fleischmann, April 3, 2006.
3. Interview with Adelbert Fleischmann, April 10, 2006.
4. *The Buffalo Evening News*, Oct. 21, 1946.
5. *The Buffalo Evening News*, Dec. 26, 1964.
6. Interview with William I. Schapiro, April 28, 2006.
7. *The Buffalo Evening News*, Aug. 11, 1969.
8. Interview with Adelbert Fleischmann, April 10, 2006.
9. Events leading up to the dedication and the dedication itself: Interview with Paul C. Weaver, May 16, 2006, and *The Buffalo News*, Aug. 9, 1983.
10. Inner office memo of May 5, 1999, signed by Albert R. Mugel.
11. Interviews with Schapiro, Weaver, and Randall Odza, May 4, 2006.
12. *The Buffalo Evening News*, June 22, 1964.
13. Ibid.
14. From *The Buffalo News* Archive, Harry J. Kelly file, 1962.
15. Interview with the Rev. Monsignor James G. Kelly, son of Harry Kelly, Sept. 8, 2006.
16. Interview with Weaver.
17. "Tribute to Harry J. Kelly," NY State Supreme Court Justice Hamilton Ward, administrative judge, 8th Judicial District, undated, 1964.
18. The Swart profile is a combination of *The Buffalo Evening News*, Feb. 7, 1966; interview with Michael Swart, son of Joseph Swart, Sept. 13, 2006; Weaver interview; Fleischmann interview, April 3, 2006.
19. Mugel's classroom descriptions are from: Weaver interview; interview with Michele O. Heffernan, June 16, 2006; Michael Swart interview; *The Buffalo News*, Sept.19, 2003; the *UB Law Review*, Fall, 2003.
20. Interview with Richard Mugel, son of Albert R. Mugel, Sept. 14, 2006.
21. Interviews with Heffernan and Weaver.
22. Interview with Odza.
23. Interview with Schapiro.
24. Ibid.
25. *From Butler to Buffett*, Murray B. Light, Prometheus Books, Amherst, N.Y., 2004, p. 195.
26. Interview with Edward G. Piwowarczyk, June 20, 2006.
27. *A Tribute to Albert R. Mugel*, Mugel National Tax Moot Court Competition, State University of New York at Buffalo web site.
28. Interview with James J. Tanous, June 6, 2006.
29. The University of Buffalo *Links*, Spring 2005.
30. Interview with John Wick, Sept. 28, 2006.
31. Interview with Walsh.
32. "John Henderson – Remembrance," by Anthony Cardinale, *The Buffalo News*, Feb. 22, 1974.
33. Interviews with Walsh and Piwowarczyk.

Chapter VII
The Sum of the Parts Times Ten

1. Interview with Randall M. Odza, May 4, 2006. Because most Chapter VII references are based on interviews referenced previously, notations will be made only when it is necessary to identity a source other than the speaker.
2. Interview with William J. Schapiro, April 28, 2006.
3. Interview with Paul C. Weaver, May 16, 2006.
4. Interview with Ralph I. Halpern, May 10, 2006.

5. Interview with Schapiro.
6. Interviews with Weaver, Odza, and Michele Heffernan, June 16, 2006.
7. Interview with Timothy Leixner, Sept. 25, 2006.
8. Interviews with Alison Fleischmann, Sept. 19, 2006, and Schapiro.
9. The *New York Times*, May 22, 1956.
10. Characterization of the Mazda-UAW agreement is from interviews with Odza and Schapiro.
11. "The World of Manly Fleischmann," by Anthony Cardinale, *The Buffalo News Magazine*, July 8, 1979.
12. Interview with Schapiro.
13. The Montfort quotation is from the interview with Odza.
14. Much of the Wagner personal information is from an interview with Anne Wagner Tierney, Larry Wagner's daughter, on Sept. 7, 2006.
15. Much of the Putnam family background is from an interview with Mrs. John G. (Thekla) Putnam on Sept. 12, 2006; the characterization of Gen. Israel Putnam is from *Fallen Founder*, Nancy Isenberg, Viking Press, 2007, pp. 33-34.
16. Stenger characterization from an interview with Edward G. Piwowarczyk, June 20, 2006.
17. Domed Stadium specifics are from "Two Olympians Go for Gold," by Ray Hill, *The Buffalo News*, Feb. 19, 1984, and *The Buffalo News*, June 15, 1989.
18. Interviews with James Tanous, June 6, 2006, and Mitchell Banas, March 26, 2007.
19. The Attica Prison Riot is capsulized from "The Rockefellers," *American Experience*, PBS-WGBH, Boston, and contemporary articles in *The Buffalo Evening News*.
20. Interview with Banas.
21. *The Buffalo News*, Oct. 22, 2003.
22. The Troy characterization is from the Heffernan and Tanous interviews.
23. Schapiro characterizations from interviews with Piwowarczyk, Tanous, Heffernan and Weaver.
24. Interview with Edward G. Piwowarczyk, April 12, 2007.

Chapter VIII
Epilogue

1. Interview with J.B. Walsh, Sept. 7, 2006.
2. Fleischmann characterization from interview with Randall M. Odza, May 4, 2006.
3. The Appellate Division incident is from interviews with Odza and Ralph L. Halpern, May 10, 2006.
4. *The Buffalo News*, March 15, 1987.
5. Interviews Alison Fleischmann, Sept. 19, 2006, and Dec. 8, 2006.
6. The eulogy for Manly Fleischmann by Albert R. Mugel, March 30, 1987.
7. From memorial service remarks by Ethan A. Hitchcock, May 13, 1987.
8. "The World of Manly Fleischmann," by Anthony Cardinale, *The Buffalo News Magazine*, July 8, 1979.
9. Interview with Odza.
10. Interview with Adelbert Fleischmann, April 10, 2006.
11. Halpern belated graduation from interview with Halpern and *The Buffalo News*, May 14, 2006.
12. Interview with Paul C. Weaver, May 16, 2006.
13. Ibid.
14. The *Buffalo Courier-Express*, Jan. 6, 1977.
15. Interview with Erma R. Jaeckle, July 28, 2006.
16. "A Lifetime in the Arena of Politics and Power," by Anthony Cardinale, *The Buffalo News Magazine*, March 2, 1980.
17. Unpublished remarks of Rupert Warren, courtesy of John L. Kirschner, Jaeckle Fleischmann archives.

Index

A.E. Anderson Family, 94
Acheson, Dean, 61
Adams, Mayor J.N., 27
Albany Office, 83, 92
Albright Art Gallery, 19, 106
Alden, Carlos, 16
Allan, Jerry, 65
Allen, Fred, 40
American Airlines, 11, 76, 96, 90, 105
American Society of Trial Lawyers, 75, 95
Amherst Office, 11, 92, 102
ArtPark, 106
Attica Prison Riot, 11, 99-100
Atwood, Charles, 69
Augspurger, Owen B. Jr., 9, 31-32, 34, 57, 70-73
Augspurger, Paula (Norris) , 31, 71
Banas, Mitchell J. Jr., 99-100
Barone, Catherine, 82
Batavia Office, 92
Battaglia, Paul A., 78
Bell Aircraft Corp., 74
Bell, Elliott V., 50, 52
Bennett High School Law Magnet, 108
Bennett, John J., 44
Bieber, Owen, 91
Black, Justice Hugo, 59-60
Blizzard of '77, 105
Board of Supervisors, 17-19
Borrelli, George, 24, 53
Bradley, Fred, 20
Bricker, Gov. John W., 47
Brosig, David, 99
Brownell, Herbert, 23, 39, 47-52
Brydges, Sen. Earl W., 106
Brydges, Thomas E., 106
Buckingham Palace, 31, 61
Buffalo & Erie County Historical Society, 72, 107
Buffalo Club, 11, 27, 45, 53, 78, 98, 107-109
Buffalo Council on World Affairs, 58
Buffalo Courier-Express, 35, 57, 97
Buffalo Evening News, 12, 20, 24, 42-45, 49, 51, 53, 64, 71-72, 97
Buffalo Maritime Heritage Assn., 100
Buffalo Medical Foundation, 74
Buffalo Philharmonic, 19, 30, 106
Buffalo Red Cross Chapter, 71
Buffalo Tennis and Squash Club, 97
Buffalo Times, 20-21

Buffett, Warren E., 12, 79-80
Burma, 11, 33
Butler, Edward H., 12, 45
Butler, Edward H. Jr., 42
Butler, Kate, 79-80
Campbell, Dwight, 57, 73-74, 101
Canisius College, 77, 81, 94, 95, 98, 100, 109
Cardinale, Anthony, 45, 49, 62
Carnegie Hall, 91
Central Avenue, Hamburg, 25
Chicago Wrecking Co., 16
Childs, Marquis, 47
Christian Radich, 100
Churchill, Winston, 46, 60
Ciminelli Development, 92
Clark, Justice Tom, 59
Cleveland, President Grover, 26-27
Cohen, Paul, 82-83
Coolidge, President Calvin, 21
Cottrell, Edward H., 97-98
Cowper Construction, 94
Cox, John, 81-82
Daniels, Bill, 27
DeCastro, J. Edmund Jr., 100
Defense Production Administration, 58
DelCotto, Louis, 81
Dewey, Gov. Thomas E., 12, 37-55
    Dapplemere farm, 40, 45
    as governor, 43-46
    growing up in Michigan, 40
    as New York prosecutor, 40-41
    presidential nominating conventions, 42-43,
       46-47, 50-52,
    run against FDR, 46-49
    run against Truman, 49-54
    at Saratoga Springs convention, 37-38
    Smith tapes, 54-55
    train engineer incident, 53
Diamond, Justice David, 76
Domed Stadium case, 11, 97-98
Donovan, Gen. William J., 30, 33
Dulles, John Foster and Allen W., 51
Dutch Schultz, 40
Eagen, Gayle L., 88, 97
EastGroup Properties, 102
Eaton, Melvin E., 21-23
Ecology & Environment, 82
Eden, Anthony, 60

Ellicott Square Building, 16, 35, 69, 73
Ellicott, Joseph, 69
Equitable Life Assurance Society, 11, 90
Estes, J Montieth (Monty), 93
Falk, Phillips, Twelvetrees & Falk, 71, 73
Fielding, David, 109
Field, Tom, 91
Fillmore, President Millard, 27
Fleischmann Commission, 62-67, 115-117
Fleischmann, Adelbert, 25, 31-32, 34-35, 90, 92,
     108-109
  with Augspurger, 32, 34-35, 70
  Blizzard of '77, 105
  growing up in Hamburg, 25, 31
  at Manly's death, 107
  marriage to Helen White, 34
  merger, 70, 85
  in World War II, 32
Fleischmann, Alison, 29-33, 57, 59-63, 89-90,
     107, 110
Fleischmann, Bianca, 28
Fleischmann, Dudley, 27, 29
Fleischmann, Edwin, 25, 27, 31
Fleischmann, Eliza (Dessauer) , 26
Fleischmann, Emanuel, 26
Fleischmann, Helen L. (White), 34, 108
Fleischmann, Justice, 27
Fleischmann, Laura (Justice), 25, 27
Fleischmann, Lawrence, 27
Fleischmann, Lois (Marseilles), 30, 60-61,
     106-108
Fleischmann, Manly, 25-35, 57-67, 105-108,
     115-117
  Buckingham Palace, 31, 61
  Blizzard of '77, 105
  with Churchill, 60
  early legal associates, 70, 73, 77, 81-82
  Education commission, 62-67, 115-117
  "The Education of Manly Fleischmann", 115
  growing up in Hamburg, 25, 28-30
  at Harvard, 29
  Lafayette Hotel, 11, 106
  marriage to Lois Marseilles, 30
  memorial services, 107-108
  Moreland study, 63
  NATO, 62
  New York law firm, 89-92
  stroke, 107
  Truman's house call, 59-60
  War Production Board, 90
  living in Washington, 33, 57-58

in World War II, 32-34
Fleischmann, Simon, 25-28
Fleischmann, Stokes & Hitchcock, 90
Ford, President Gerald R., 88
Frauenheim Foundation, 76
Fruit Belt, 10, 15, 19, 24, 87, 110
Fuzak, Victor T., 98
Gannett, Frank, 42
Gardner, Sunderland (Sonny), 87-88
Garono, Edward J., 16, 17, 69, 75
German-American Bank, 86, 87
Grand Central Hotel, 37, 38
Greater Buffalo Development Foundation, 71
Greene, Justice Manly, 28
Griffin, Mayor Jimmy, 73
Hagerty, James C., 50
Halpern, Ralph L., 16, 18, 54, 86, 89, 109
Harper's Magazine, 28, 29, 58
Hauptman-Woodward Foundation, 74
Heffernan, Michele O., 78, 87, 88, 89, 96, 106, 109
Henderson, Judge John O., 57, 65, 67, 82, 101
Hens & Kelly, 74
Herman, Mario, 92
Hickey, William J., 20
Hill, Bully, 37, 42
Hill, Ray, 98
Hilton, Conrad, 12
Hitchcock, Ethan A., 63, 90, 108
Holling, Thomas F., 21
Hoover, President Herbert, 21
Hotel Roosevelt, 45
Hotel Touraine, 18
Hughes, Stephen B., 92
Hyatt Regency Hotel, 89
Internationl Railway Corp. (IRC), 12, 74
Jaeckle, Erma Hallett, 49, 110
Jaeckle, Grace F. (Drechsel), 18-19, 75, 110
Jaeckle, Jacob, 15
Jaeckle, Mary (Marx), 15-16
Jaeckle, Edwin F., 15-24, 37-55, 108-112, 114
  Buffalo Club, 11, 45, 53, 108, 109
  Chicago Convention of 1944, 46-48
  Dewey presidential runs, 42-43, 46-49, 50-54
   early legal associates, 16, 19, 70, 74-76, 81, 82
  Erie County chairman, 20-21
  growing up in Fruit Belt, 10, 15-16, 19
  hit by car, 111
  Dewey loss to Truman, 49-54
  marriages, 18-19, 110
  Nixon visit, 110
   Philadelphia Convention of 1940, 42-43

Philadelphia Convention of 1948, 50-52
race for mayor of Buffalo, 21
reconciliation with Dewey, 51
resignation in 1944, 48
retire to Florida, 111
Roswell Park Cancer Institute, 45
running the state Legislature, 45
Saratoga Springs convention, 37
Smith tapes, 54-55
state GOP chairman, 39
Victory Special, 52-53
Young Turks, 21, 23, 39
Jensen, Ronald H., 78, 81
Jones-Rich Milk, 71
Justice, William G., 27
Kavanaugh, Cyril, 81, 82
Kelly, Harry J., 16, 74-76, 95
Kelly, Helen (Madigan), 75
Kelly, Mayor Joseph, 75
Kelly, Msgr. James G., 75
Kensington Expressway, 15, 95, 105
Kirchhofer, Alfred H., 42-46, 48, 51
Kisicki, Ronald, 93
Klein, Peter G., 94
Kovacs, William L., 92
Kubarek, Joseph P., 102
Ladd, Carlton E., 16, 20
LaFalce, Congressman John J., 109
Laidlaw, Archibald, 87
Lake Erie Tractions Line, 27
Landon, Alf M., 39-40, 42
Laudenbach, the Rev., 17
Lehman, Gov. Herbert H., 38-39, 44
Leixner, Timothy, 78, 89
Lemon Street, 11, 15, 17, 87, 95
Lend Lease, 33
Lenzner Corp., 76
Liberty Bank, 62, 72, 75, 87-89, 105
Liggett & Myers, 91
Light, Murray B., 79
Lindsay, Mayor John, 90
Lipsey, Stanford, 80
Loblaws grocery chain, 76
Lockwood, Paul E., 50, 53
Loftis, Tim C., 94
Lord Mountbatten Indian Ocean Theater, 33
Love Canal, 11, 97
Luce, Clare Booth, 54
Lucky Luciano, 40
MacArthur, Gen. Douglas, 51
Main Place Mall, 72
Marseilles, Ione, 82

Masten Park High School, 15, 111
Mayo Clinic, 111
Mazda, 91
McKinley, President William, 16, 72, 89
Meddoff, Jack, 20, 38, 43, 49
Merchants Mutual, 71
Meyer Malt, 76
Middle Atlantic Warehouse, 94
Millard Fillmore Hospital, 103, 107
Monahan, Major John, 99
Montfort, John M., 78, 85, 94-95, 101
Moore, Frank C., 45
Moore, James O., 33
Moot, Adelbert, 25
Morehouse, L. Judson, 108
Moreland study, 63
Moses, Robert, 37
Mount Calvary Cemetery, 95-96
Mugel, Albert R., 74, 77-81, 90, 93, 96-97,
    102, 107
Murray, William S., 23, 39
National Production Authority, 57-58
NATO, 62
NFT, NFTA, 12, 74
Neville, Paul E., 97
New York State Thruway, 95
New York Times, 21-23, 38, 39, 42, 45, 48-50,
    64-67, 115-117
Newman Family, 94
Niagara Mohawk Power, 81
Nichols School, 31, 32, 70, 97
Nixon, President Richard M., 110
NOCO, 94
Norton, Lee, 72
O'Brian, John Lord, 30, 33, 57, 70, 108
Odza, Randall M., 42, 48, 54, 62-63, 67, 78, 80,
    86, 89, 91, 106, 108, 111
Office of Production Management, 32
Oishei Foundation, 78
Old Orchard Inn, 108
Olsen, Nils, 80
Oswald, Russell G., 99
Palmer, Hauck & Wickser, 16
Palmer, Thomas A., 78, 94, 102
Pan American Exposition, 16, 27, 88
Park, Dr. Roswell, 45
Parkway Properties, 102
Pfeil, Karl, 99-100
Phoenix Office, 93
Piwowarczyk, Edward G., 80, 83, 89, 95, 103, 106
Pooley, Maj. Gen. William R., 26
Powers, Jean C., 88, 94, 96

Public School 37, 16
Putnam, Gen. Israel, 96
Putnam, John G. Jr., 30, 78-79, 96-97, 101
Putnam, Thekla (Mrs. John G.) , 30, 96-97
Queen Elizabeth, 61
Raichle, Frank G., 86. 106
Rand Building, 20, 69-70, 81-82, 87, 97
Roblin-Seaway Industries, 71
Rochester Office, 11, 93
Rockefeller, Gov. Nelson A., 45, 62-63, 65, 99, 106, 108
Roosevelt, President Franklin D., 20, 32, 39-40, 43, 46, 49-50, 53, 54, 88.
Roosevelt, President Theodore, 72
Rosary Hill College, 19
Rosenhoch, Howard S., 96
Rosse, Lillian, 53
Roswell Park Cancer Institute, 45
Rothstein, Julius, 38
Rubenstein, Susan, 102
Sage Equipment, 76
Saturn Club, 97
Sawyer, Commissioner Charles, 58-59
Schapiro, William I., 5-6, 23, 46, 53, 63, 67, 72, 74, 78, 85, 90-91, 101-102
Schelling, Robert F., 16
Schmidt, Leo, 17-18, 20
Schmidt, Peter J., 89
Schoellkopf Power Station, 81
Schutz, R.J. (Chris), 72
Sears, Judge Charles B., 29
Seneca Foods, 102
Sidney Blumenthal Co., 90
Simpson, Kenneth S., 37, 42-43
Sirica, Judge John J., 111
Smith, Gov. Alfred E., 20
Smith, Frank (Big Black), 99
Smith, H. Catherine, 35
Smith, Richard Norton, 40-41, 43, 46, 48, 53, 54
Spink, E. Perry, 87
Sprague, J. Russel, 23, 44, 47, 52
St. John's-Grace Episcopal Church, 97
St. Louis Church, 17, 19
St. Peter's Church, 15
Stassen, Harold E., 47
Statler Hotel, 12, 82
Stenger, John H., 11, 95, 97-100, 106
Sterling Amherst Farms Dairy, 75
Sterling Engine Co., 58
Swados, Robert, 83
Swart, Joseph, 16, 74, 76-77, 101
Swart, Michael, 76

Sweet, George C. (Clint), 87-88
Szymczak, Heath J., 108
Taft, Robert, 47
Talbott, Paul E., 50
Tanous, James J., 80, 85, 89, 92, 93, 97, 102-103, 110
Tedards, William P. Jr., 92
Temple Beth Zion, 28
Tennessee Waltz, (Patti Page), 60
Theodore Roosevelt Inaugural Site, 72
Time Magazine, 47, 52, 59, 64
Trico Products, 78
Troy, Brian J., 101
Troy, Norma (Alesii), 101
Truman, President Harry S., 12, 50, 53, 57-58, 60, 62
Turner, Douglas, 97
UB Law Forum, 17
UB Law School, 16, 29, 71, 74, 76, 80, 87, 96, 98, 100, 108, 109
Ulrich, Charles, 19, 20
Uncle Sams, 43
Unitarian Universalist Church, 27
United Auto Workers, 91
United Way of Buffalo & Erie County, 71
Victory Special, 52, 53
Wagner, Lawrence H., 17, 95-96
Wall, Carl, 22
Walsh, J.B., 69, 70, 81-82, 92, 105
Wanakah Country Club, 88
War Production Board, 90
Ward, Justice Hamilton, 76
Warren, Gov. Earl, 47, 52
Warren, Ruppert, 112
Washington Office, 92
Washington Post, 47, 62
Waxey Gordon, 40
Weaver, Paul C., 54, 73, 75-76, 78, 87, 105, 110
Webster & Sheffield, 63, 90-92, 107-108
Wendt, Daniel E., 89
White, Robert, 82
Wick Charles J., 16, 81
Wick, John, 17, 70, 81
Wilcox & Van Allen, 72, 87
Willkie, Wendell, 43, 46, 111
Wilson, Ralph C., 97
Yellen, Maury and Jack, 90
Yokich, Steven, 91
Young Turks, 21, 23, 39